# Osama bin Laden

## A War Against the West

**ELAINE LANDAU**

TWENTY-FIRST CENTURY BOOKS
BROOKFIELD, CONNECTICUT

Published by Twenty-First Century Books
A Division of The Millbrook Press, Inc.
2 Old New Milford Road
Brookfield, Connecticut 06804
www.millbrookpress.com

Library of Congress Cataloging-in-Publication Data
Landau, Elaine.
Osama bin Laden : a war against the West / Elaine Landau.
p. cm.
Includes bibliographical references and index.
Summary: Presents biographical information about militant Islamic leader
Osama bin Laden, including his role in international terrorism and the
beliefs that fuel his actions.
ISBN 0-7613-1709-0 (lib. bdg.)
1. Bin Laden, Osama, 1957– . 2. Terrorists—Biography—Juvenile litera-
ture. 3. Terrorism—Juvenile literature. [1. Bin Laden, Osama, 1957– . 2.
Terrorists.] 4. Terrorism—Religious aspects—Islam.] I. Title.
HV6430.B55 L36 2002
322.4'2'-092—dc21  [B]  2001041465

Photographs courtesy of AP/Wide World Photos: pp. 6, 8, 52, 124;
TimePix: p. 16 (© Andrees Latif/Reuters); Sygma: pp. 26, 82; Liaison
Agency: pp. 38 (© Robert Nickelsberg), 110 (© Steven Daniel); Gamma
Presse US: p. 66 (© P. Aventurier); © AFP/Corbis: p. 92

# Contents

*It is clear from this poster, for sale in Pakistan in 1999, that Osama bin Laden is a hero to his followers.*

# A Note From the Author

I began writing about Osama bin Laden in 1998. At the time he had just been implicated as the mastermind in the bombings of two U.S. embassies in Africa. Bin Laden had carried out these sinister acts with chilling precision and it was obvious that he was on the verge of becoming an even more powerful force in international terrorism.

Obtaining accurate information on an internationally wanted terrorist such as Osama bin Laden can be challenging for any writer. While continuing to elude authorities, bin Laden has frequently shifted his hideouts as his supporters deliberately generate misinformation about his whereabouts, tactics, and goals. It was especially difficult to find accurate data regarding Osama bin Laden's personal life, and on more than one occasion, conflicting facts have caused bin Laden to be referred to as "a fact checker's nightmare."

Despite the difficulties involved, my publisher and I felt it was important to know more about Osama bin Laden and we continued this project. Just as we were putting the finishing touches on the manuscript, a horrendous four-pronged terrorist assault on U.S. soil was launched, and bin Laden quickly became the prime suspect. We now believe that it is more important than ever to understand the forces that propel Osama bin Laden and his international terrorist organization. We have tried to bring you a look at a man at the forefront of a violent political movement that has significantly impacted our world.

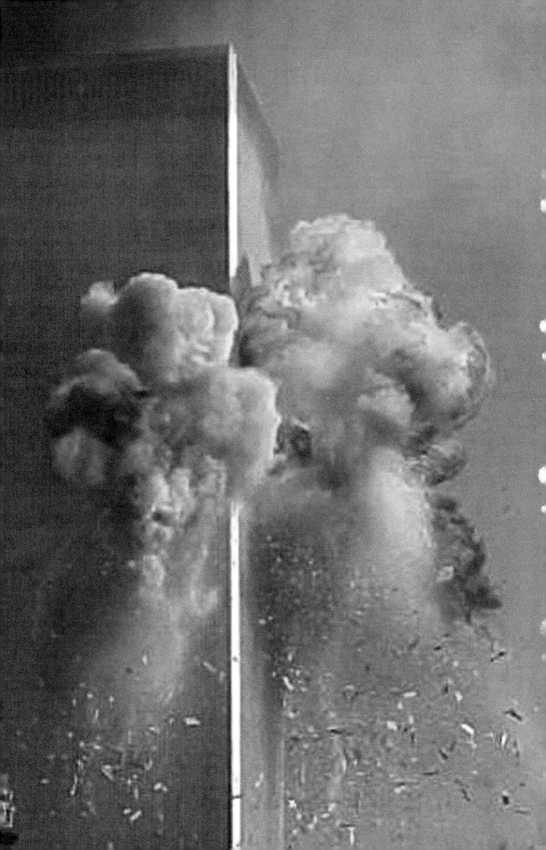

# Attack on
# America

Tuesday...September 11, 2001...8:30 A.M.

A busy workday was about to start at New York City's World Trade Center. Since 1972 the World Trade Center had been the city's tallest skyscraper. Located on 16 acres, it had twin towers that rose to a height of 1,350 feet. Yet the World Trade Center was more than just a fabulous part of New York City's skyline. The Center had a railroad station, hotel, and other facilities. About 50,000 people worked there daily and an additional 150,000 people visited it each year. The World Trade Center stood as a symbol of

*A fireball explodes from one of the World Trade Center towers after a jet airliner crashed into the building on the morning of Tuesday, September 11, 2001, in New York City.*

**9**

American business and achievement. It was a towering landmark that reflected the United States at its best.

Perhaps that is why it no longer exists. The Center was destroyed on September 11, 2001. The carnage began at 8:48 A.M., when a hijacked American Airlines commercial jet headed for California crashed into the World Trade Center's North Tower. There was an explosion and the tower burst into flames. When the plane disappeared from the sky, a witness said that it looked as if the building had swallowed up the aircraft. But that was just the start of a day of terror.

At 9:03 A.M. a hijacked United Airlines passenger jet, also bound for California, rammed into the South Tower at the World Trade Center. Now both buildings were burning. It was a horrendous blaze since each of the hijacked planes carried a large amount of fuel for their scheduled coast-to-coast flights. Now the extra fuel made the fires particularly intense.

The area began to look like a full-blown war zone. Lower Manhattan was soon covered with a dense curtain of smoke. Gray powdery debris was strewn throughout the area. The streets were filled with people trying to escape the fire while avoiding the falling shards of glass and the moving wall of smoke that seemed to chase them. Others never made it out of the towers. Some fell or jumped from the windows to their deaths.

Witnesses to the tragedy felt as if they had seen the unimaginable. "I don't know what the gates of hell look like, but it's got to look like this," noted John Maloney, a security director for an Internet firm at the World Trade Center. "I'm a combat veteran, Vietnam, and I never saw anything like this."[1]

About forty minutes later at 9:45 A.M. terror struck for a third time. This strike took place in Washington, D.C. Another hijacked airliner was spearheaded into the Pentagon. The nation's military headquarters–the symbol of U.S. prowess and might–had been attacked. A huge smoke plume towered over the building and it wasn't long before a portion of the structure collapsed. Evacuation had begun immediately but unfortunately that was still too late for many.

Hope was quickly fading at the World Trade Center as well. It was obvious that the death toll would be in the thousands. The scorching heat affected the towers' steel beams which only hours ago had seemed impenetrable. By noon both of the World Trade Center's towers had collapsed. These 110-story build-ings were reduced to a huge pile of steel and concrete. A famed American landmark had been wiped off the map. Yet the overall destruction proved to be far more massive. It was estimated that the attack had caused ten blocks of damage in every direction. The Federal Bureau of Investigation (FBI) later described the area as the largest crime scene ever on United States soil.

The nation already ached but there was more to come. A fourth plane was hijacked. A United Airlines flight from Newark, New Jersey, to San Francisco was also diverted from its destination. The plane crashed just outside of Pittsburgh, Pennsylvania. It was later revealed that the White House and the presidential plane Air Force One had been among the other possible targets slated for that day.

Terrorists had attacked the world's last superpower. Some said that the day's events had been too improbable for a Hollywood screenplay. Yet they happened. The terrorists struck at symbols of U.S. financial and military might. Americans were stunned by the magnitude, sophistication, and precision of the assault. Many wondered if life in the U.S. would ever be quite the same. No one believed that this could have happened here.

Newspaper headlines throughout the nation read "U.S. ATTACKED!" Arguably, it felt as if the country were at war. But this enemy was far more elusive than another nation. Government officials soon concluded that the attack had been planned and ordered by Osama bin Laden—a man fervently against the United States. As is typical of bin Laden, about three weeks prior to the assault, he noted that the United States would soon be attacked in an unprecedented way. The warning was vague, but that is bin Laden's style. True to form, after the attack bin Laden denied having anything to do with it. That is his style, too. U.S. officials have come to expect this and the frustration it engenders.

Osama bin Laden has been called the world's most dangerous terrorist. A grand jury indictment refers to him as the head of a global terrorist organization willing to use any means necessary to drive U.S. forces permanently from the Persian Gulf region. The Central Intelligence Agency (CIA) believes that since the mid-1990s, Osama bin Laden has been associated with every major Muslim terrorist organization in the world. He has frequently been described as "the godfather of radical Islamic views" and remains on the U.S.'s ten-most-wanted list.[2] Although the United States had a $25 million price on his head, he was not turned in.

Who is Osama bin Laden? His followers see him as a religious hero, while others view him as a treacherous murderer. What we do know about Osama bin Laden sets him apart from others who rally to the same cause. Bin Laden is a multimillionaire from Saudi Arabia who gave up comfort and wealth to lead armed Islamic militants in an international holy war. He traded a life of ease to carry out his plans from barren hideaways in the mountain caves of southern Afghanistan. Bin Laden claims to have been motivated by his religious beliefs. Yet his views in no way reflect those of the vast majority of Muslims. Like most religious and law-abiding people around the globe, they find his philosophy and actions incomprehensible.

How did Osama bin Laden become a leader in an ongoing holy war against Americans and Jews throughout the world? His story lies within these pages. It is the saga of a man who, as early as 1998, warned America: "The battle has not yet started!"3

# 2

# A
# Man at War

IT IS IMPOSSIBLE TO UNDERSTAND Osama bin Laden without examining the religious beliefs and fervor that have shaped his life and that fuel his present actions. Osama bin Laden is a Muslim who, like all Muslims, believes that Allah, or God, is the lord of the universe. Like all Muslims, bin Laden views the Koran, the Muslim holy book, as containing all the knowledge necessary to live a life of faith and arrive at the gates of paradise at death. Among other activities, the Koran expressly forbids adultery, gambling, cheating, drinking alcohol, eating pork, and lending money at interest.

Muslims are required to place worship and obedience to Allah above all else and bin Laden claims to do

so. Yet this may be where much of the similarity between Osama bin Laden's view of Islam and that of the vast majority of Muslims end. Millions of Muslims throughout the world believe they dutifully follow Islam's teachings, but radical Islamic militants, like Osama bin Laden, strongly disagree. They reject popular interpretations of Islamic law as being far too permissive. These fundamentalists interpret the Koran in its strictest sense, which leads them to view the United States, for example, as a corrupt and ungodly country, where the pursuit of money and immoral pleasures rules.

The militant fundamentalists do not want Western corruption to infect the Muslim world. Bin Laden and other extremists support the notion that the U.S. presence in the Middle East has long prevented Islamic fundamentalist governments, which would interpret the Koran in its strictest sense, from rising to power. They feel that due to U.S. support, less devout Muslim regimes, sympathetic to U.S. business and political interests, have remained in place.

Regarding the United States, with its modern ways and international involvements, as the chief enemy of their faith, Islamic militants have pledged to drive the enemy out. On a number of occasions since 1998, Osama bin Laden declared war against the United

*Hundreds of thousands of Muslims pray at Mecca in this 2001 photograph.*

States and encouraged his followers to do the same. This struggle is a holy war known as a jihad. The Islamic militants' concept of an ongoing jihad is international in scope. Any country where there is a significant Muslim population is considered part of the larger all encompassing Islamic nation and therefore they believe must be purged of Western influence and domination.

This view was expressed by a leading Iraqi Shiite scholar Ayatollah Muhammed Baqir al-Sadr when he noted, "The world as it is today is how others [that is, non-Muslims] shape it. We have two choices: either to accept it with submission, which means letting Islam die, or to destroy it, so that we can construct the world as Islam requires."[1]

These feelings were underscored by Abdul-Qadir as Sufi ad-Darqawi, who is considered one of the greatest interpreters of contemporary Islamic fundamentalist thinking. "We are at war," he stressed. "And our battle has only just begun. Our first victory will be one track of land somewhere in the world that is under the complete rule of Islam. Islam is moving across the earth. Nothing can stop [its] spreading in Europe and America."[2]

Since Muslim nations are not in a military or financial position to challenge a superpower like the United States on a conventional battlefield, the militants' jihad employs less direct but often extremely effective tac-

tics. One Islamic theorist described the way jihad must
be waged in today's world:

> Jihad is not confined to the summoning of
> troops and the establishment of huge forces.
> It takes various forms. From all the territories
> of Islam there should arise a group of people
> reinforced with faith, well equipped with
> means and methods; and then let them set
> out to attack the usurpers [the United States]
> harassing them incessantly until their abode
> is one of everlasting torment. . . . Jihad will
> never end. . . . It will last to the Day of
> Judgment."[3]

These militant religious fighters are often referred to
as jihadists, though much of the world views them as
terrorists. This includes the U.S. government, which
has been forced to fight an often elusive terrorist
enemy. Unlike in traditional warfare, jihadist strikes
are often sudden and anonymous.

It is important to stress that Osama bin Laden's
view of jihad differs sharply from that held by the
larger Muslim community. Most Muslims regard the
idea of a warlike jihad as a Western misconception.
They stress that there are two jihads—a "greater jihad"
and a "lesser jihad." The "greater jihad" is the ongoing
struggle to fight the evil within oneself. Its essence lies

in the believer's personal quest to be true to the faith. The "lesser jihad" is secondary and is supposedly a war waged only against a direct threat to the religion. In explaining the difference, Muslims sometimes quote a story in which the prophet Muhammad said, "Look, the fight against the enemy was but the 'Lesser Jihad,' now that we have won this battle we have to begin with the 'Greater Jihad' that is, the fight against the enemy within ourselves, the battle for self-purification."[4]

The jihadists, or Islamic extremists, do not distinguish between a greater and lesser jihad. For them, jihad is a call to arms to ensure that foreign powers are expelled from Muslim domains at any cost. It is also a directive to force all Muslims to submit to the true essence of Islam as interpreted by the fundamentalists. Bin Laden himself has been quoted as saying, "Killing Americans and their allies, civilian and military is an individual duty for every Muslim." Yet as one former CIA analyst noted, "He [bin Laden] is driven by his extremist version of Islam which is far, far removed from the voices of authentic Islam."[5]

Bin Laden's role in this holy war cannot be underestimated. He is an important leader in the struggle, whose violent acts have set an example for those with similar beliefs to follow. Osama bin Laden is a frightening hero because of the effectiveness of so many of his undertakings. He's also especially intimidating, since unlike many terrorist group leaders in the past, he has a sizable following.

Osama bin Laden has never been an isolated rene-
gade. Instead, he rose to a position of respect and
power within a well-organized international terrorist
network based in the Middle East. It's a network that
includes expert bomb makers, intelligence gatherers, an
elaborate training system, weapons stashes, and loyal
soldiers. In addition, states within the Muslim world
that share bin Laden's fundamentalist views along with
his hatred for the West have often provided both
funding and sanctuary to help him achieve his objectives. It's nothing short of state-sponsored terrorism.

Bin Laden's ultimate goal—the establishment of
Islamic fundamentalist governments throughout the
world—is the dream of his many followers. To some
degree that type of regime has been operational in
Afghanistan, where for some time, Osama bin Laden
has effectively avoided U.S. attempts to apprehend
him. The Taliban, an Islamic extremist group, has long
admired bin Laden and provided sanctuary for him.
Since seizing control of about 85 percent of
Afghanistan in 1996, it has vowed to restore "the
purity of Islam" there. For the Taliban this has meant
outlawing just about everything that could distract
Afghan citizens from their religion, including movies,
picnics, wedding celebrations, music festivals, and any
other type of gathering in which men and women who
are not relatives might mix.

The Taliban established a Ministry of Religion
along with a minister for "the prevention of vice and

the promotion of virtue." It was this individual, Mohammed Qalamuddin, who in the late 1990s gave the people of Afghanistan fifteen days to dispose of their TVs before the religious police would come to their homes to smash the sets. Videocassette recorders, videotapes, and satellite dishes were also banned. Minister Qalamuddin has frequently referred to television and videos as the root of corruption in society.

The only movie theater in Kabul, the country's capital, was shut down, and books, newspapers, and magazines published outside Afghanistan are forbidden. Other banned items include children's toys, playing cards, board games, cameras, cigarettes, and alcohol.

Music and art shared a similar fate. Every type of music except religious songs was declared off limits. Taliban soldiers vandalized the country's only radio station, destroying its entire music collection. They broke open audio cassettes of private citizens as well, pulling out the tapes, which they strung over fence posts throughout the countryside. The religious police also routinely stop cars to search for any hidden music tapes.

The Koran forbids the worship of idols, and the Taliban used this to justify the destruction of priceless Buddhist sculptures made prior to the Muslims' arrival in the eighth century. This included a 175-foot-high sculpture said to be the biggest standing Buddha in the world. In addition, the contents of a number of museums were destroyed.

These regulations are not germane to either Afghanistan or Islam. As a U.S. press correspondent described the situation, "The extremism espoused by [Islamic fundamentalists] such as bin Laden represents a form of Islam totally alien to Afghan tradition, culture, and religion. Music and dance, for example, have always been part of Afghan life yet they are now banned by the Taliban . . . In the remaining non-Taliban areas such dictates are considered absurd."[6]

"Whatever we are doing in our country, it is not in order for the world to be happy with us," noted the former Taliban deputy minister of foreign affairs, Sher Abbas Stanakzai. "Time should be spent serving the country and praying to God. Nothing else. Everything else is a waste of time, and people are not allowed to waste time."[7]

Many of the Taliban's restrictions are especially hard on women. Though they say their actions are based on the Koran, many would disagree. Most Muslims claim that none of the teachings of Islam sanction the Taliban's deeds. It's been argued that the Taliban's treatment of women is based more on a male-dominated culture than on religion. In any case, they closed schools for girls, and women were no longer permitted to work outside the home. It is illegal to wear makeup, nail polish, high-heeled shoes, or colorful clothing.

Women are forced to wear a garment known as a *burqa*, which completely covers them from head to foot. The veiled women can see only through a heavy patch of gauze fabric that covers their eyes. Compelled to wear a *burqa*, a number of women have been hit by cars since their peripheral vision is completely blocked. Such restrictive dress also prevents them from walking quickly to avoid oncoming cars.

Yet dodging traffic is not a great concern for Afghanistan's women, since they are not permitted to leave their homes unless accompanied by a male relative. One Taliban edict actually reads: "Women, you should not step outside your residence."[8] The government has further mandated that all windows on the first floor of homes be painted black to prevent anyone from looking in at the women inside.

Religious police continually patrol the streets ensuring that Taliban regulations are adhered to. In many cases these are teenage boys who have been armed with automatic weapons. They also carry broken-off car antennae or electric cabling with which to beat any women they determine are not properly obeying the regulations.

Punishments under the Taliban's rule can be far worse, however. A thief might have his right hand publicly amputated, while a woman can receive a hundred lashes for walking with a man to whom she is not related. Women suspected of adultery are publicly stoned to death.

Amnesty International, the human rights organization, has referred to the Taliban's rule in Afghanistan as "a human rights catastrophe."[9] Yet Osama bin Laden considers the men of the Taliban his brothers. They have created and maintained an Islamic fundamentalist state ensuring a way of life that he wants to see spread throughout the Muslim world. It's a goal that Osama bin Laden and others like him are willing to fight and die for. While these individuals represent only a very small slice of the world's Muslims, their determination and zeal are chilling.

# 3
# In the Beginning

OSAMA BIN LADEN WAS NOT BROUGHT UP to be a Muslim extremist. When he was born in 1957 in the city of Riyadh, Saudi Arabia, his future looked bright. No one could have guessed that he'd spend much of his adult life waging a holy war against the West.

The bin Ladens were a large brood. Osama's father, Mohammed bin Laden, was a builder and contractor, who during his lifetime had eleven wives and at least fifty-two children. Osama's mother, his father's eleventh bride, was a petite Syrian woman. It had been rumored that she was his least favorite wife and that was why her husband had only one child with her. If

*Osama bin Laden in a 1998 photograph*

that was the case, however, it never seemed to dampen his enthusiasm for Osama, his seventeenth son. The boy was included in all family gatherings and outings.

Mohammed bin Laden was an ambitious man with a natural flair for business. He had brought his family from Yemen to Saudi Arabia with the hope of enhancing both his professional standing and the opportunities afforded his children. Things worked out even better than the elder bin Laden had anticipated, as the area's oil boom provided a lucrative environment for the building industry. Mohammed bin Laden readily turned social relationships into business deals and managed to forge enduring bonds with many of the well-to-do members of Saudi society. This included ties to members of the house of al-Saud—Saudi Arabia's ruling family.

The bin Laden Construction Corporation grew to be one of the largest and most profitable construction enterprises in the Middle East. It built mosques (Muslim houses of worship), airports, roads, and a wide range of facilities at the bidding of the Saudi ruling elite. Mohammed bin Laden also undertook projects for the governing heads of other Arab states.

The strength of Mohammed bin Laden's bond with the Saudi royal family was instrumental to his ultimate success. On numerous occasions he used whatever money and influence he acquired to bolster the image of the house of al-Saud and was richly rewarded for his loyalty. At one point when the Saudi treasury had reached a low ebb, he paid the country's civil servants for several months. In return, King Faisal later decreed that all of the nation's construction contracts would be awarded to bin Laden's company. Mohammed bin Laden even served as the minister of public works for a brief time.

When Osama bin Laden's father died in a plane crash in 1967, King Faisal reportedly felt the loss deeply. Osama would later say, "King Faisal said upon the death of my father that today I have lost my right hand."[1]

Even after Mohammed bin Laden's death, the house of al-Saud continued to patronize generously the bin Laden Construction Corporation, which was taken over by some of bin Laden's sons. By the mid-1990s the company's estimated worth was $36 billion. At that point the company had further diversified internationally. It was involved in telecommunications, the import/export business, and other lucrative areas of trade. Some people say that the bin Ladens are to Saudi Arabia what the Rockefellers were to the West.

Yet despite his financial success, Mohammed bin Laden had led a deeply religious life and made certain that his children were raised as devout Muslims. A business associate of Osama's father described the man's religious zeal as follows:

"He was fascinated—obsessed—by religion. He loved obscure religious debates and spent huge sums financing these regular evening meetings called 'halqas' where the greatest preachers and religious leaders in the Saudi Kingdom would gather to debate theology. I guess it satisfied some philosophical streak in him."[2]

While he was growing up, it looked as though Osama bin Laden would eventually take his place in the family business. In fact, through much of their early life, he and his brothers were groomed for it. After successfully completing high school, Osama furthered his education at King Abdul Aziz University, which was considered one of the finest institutions of higher learning in Saudi Arabia. There he studied economics and management with an eye to a future in business. Osama also learned the behind-the-scenes dynamics of his family's enterprise. He read company reports and attended business meetings.

Although Osama studied in the Middle East at a school steeped in Muslim tradition, most of his brothers chose to attend universities abroad where they enjoyed the freedom of Western culture. This was particularly true of Osama's half bother Salim—Mohammed bin Laden's firstborn and favorite son. Salim, known for his good looks and charm, was educated in London. He flew his own private plane and had a reputation as a playboy.

That's not to say that in the early 1970s, Osama did not exhibit some of the same tendencies. Like many young men from affluent and influential Saudi families, Osama was somewhat of a pleasure seeker. Alone, as well as with groups of friends, he was known to make the trip to Beirut, Lebanon, regularly to savor the excitement of that city's fast-paced nightlife. It was not unusual for him to spend hours frequenting the bars, nightclubs, and gambling casinos. He often drank and sometimes consumed more alcohol than he should have. Bin Laden also enjoyed the company of beautiful women and spent time with numerous young ladies during this period in his life. A U.S. intelligence agent looking into bin Laden's background described his behavior as follows: "Those who knew him [Osama bin Laden] when he was in Beirut all said the same thing. He was spending cash in clubs and bars. He drank quantities of alcohol, [he was] a binge-drinker, and he had an eye for the ladies."[3] It was further noted that on several occasions Osama bin Laden became involved in barroom brawls over women, one of whom was a well-known prostitute in the area.

Often men with Osama bin Laden's money and advantages continued this lifestyle indefinitely, but this wasn't so for Osama. As it happened, he would undergo a spiritual rebirth causing him to turn to Islam with fervent devotion that eventually altered his goals and lifestyle dramatically.

"It's a classic thing," a bin Laden family friend said in describing Osama's transformation:

> They [wealthy young Saudis] have all this money and they think they are kings of the world, and they start spending money like

water. As soon as they leave Saudi Arabia,
they forget their religion. They would go to
Beirut and buy whores and get drunk, and
then eventually have this religious crisis—and
some of the young [bin Laden] brothers
became very religious. I remember one of the
brothers went off and spent weeks praying in
the desert.[4]

Osama bin Laden's metamorphosis didn't occur
overnight. First he worked on restoring two mosques,
which made him feel closer to Allah as he began to
contemplate a holier way of life. Bin Laden also started
meeting with Islamic fundamentalists and reading
more about the teachings of Islam. His trips to Beirut
were finished by 1975, when this formerly sparkling
city was turned into a combat zone by a civil war in
which Christians and Muslims were pitted against one
another. Islamic fundamentalists in Saudi Arabia
openly blamed the city's devastation on the fast and
loose lifestyle of the Muslims there and, in time, bin
Laden felt inclined to agree. By then he had settled
down and become a devout Muslim. He agreed to an
arranged marriage with an equally devout Syrian
woman who was a distant cousin.

The upheaval in the Middle East during the 1970s
was another force that drove Osama bin Laden closer
to Islamic fundamentalism. In 1973 the defeat of the
Arab states by Israel in the Yom Kippur War sent a

crushing blow to regional Muslim pride. The United States, viewed as Israel's most influential backer against the surrounding belligerent Arab states, lent support to the pervasive image of the United States as the enemy.

Osama bin Laden, along with many other affluent Muslims, was no longer impressed by much of what he saw in Western society. The promiscuity, blatant drug and alcohol abuse, along with the breakdown of the family and society, were not things he wished to see emulated in his part of the world. These sentiments were reinforced by the assassination of Saudi Arabia's King Faisal by his deranged nephew. The king's nephew, who was educated in the United States, spent much of his time in Europe and had become completely westernized. As the nation mourned the death of a very popular ruler, Islamic fundamentalists seized the opportunity to argue that the king's nephew had become polluted by Western vice in defiance of Allah's teachings.

Young Saudis like Osama bin Laden who had seriously begun to question Western values and priorities were offered an alternative by the Islamic fundamentalist preachers and teachers who had taken refuge in the mosques and universities of the Middle East during this period. These intellectual leaders made it clear that the only way to avoid Western corruption and expel this enemy from the Muslim world was to revert to Islam in its strictest sense.

Many felt encouraged by the events that occurred in Iran in 1979. There, a fundamentalist religious leader known as Ayatollah Ruhollah Khomeni overthrew the ruling shah who was considered a close ally of the United States as well as a leader who had put nonreligious culture before the true practice of Islam. For the first time, Islamic fundamentalists had seized a Muslim country and established an Islamic state. It was viewed as a significant victory over the United States, Western vice, and spiritual pollution. Perhaps, more importantly, it stood as undeniable proof that radical Islamic forces could prevail.

The Islamic revolution in Iran was a source of pride and inspiration to Islamic fundamentalists in Egypt, Lebanon, and Iraq. This movement, based on a strict return to Islamic teachings, gained strength and followers in these nations and the fervor spread to Saudi Arabia, where Osama bin Laden was evolving into an ardent follower.

Yet the event that fully radicalized bin Laden and thousands of other young Muslims occurred toward the end of 1979 when the former Soviet Union invaded the largely Muslim nation of Afghanistan. The Soviet Union was a dominant world power prior to the fall of communism and the nation's breakup in 1991. In 1979 the Soviets were still anxious to spread communism and annex new territory. They'd been supporting a pro-Soviet government in Afghanistan but felt their grip on the country loosen when that regime began to be seriously challenged by Islamic fundamentalists in neighboring Pakistan.

To secure the area and quell the growing wave of Islamic extremism, the Soviets marched in, killed the president in power, and established their own governmental head. It was the first time in over thirty-five years that a non-Islamic country had taken over a Muslim nation and the action outraged the entire Muslim world. It also left a pressing question to be answered: Who in the region was prepared to fight the Soviets for Islam?

It was soon obvious that the Middle Eastern Arab nations did not feel capable of taking on a world power like the Soviet Union. Yet they were well aware that the Soviet presence in Afghanistan provided a "too close for comfort" base from which a well-equipped Soviet attack against them could readily be launched. As Professor Richard Pipes, director of East European and Soviet Affairs for the United Nations (UN) National Security Council summed up the predicament, "The Soviet shadow over this area looms so large that many Muslim regimes cannot find the courage to challenge it; the more savagely the Russians deal with the Afghan resistance, the greater the dread they strike into the hearts of other Muslim countries."[5]

While sympathetic Muslim nations dared not openly assist their fellow Muslims under Soviet domination, Islamic fundamentalist militants reacted differently. Ousting the Soviets and restoring Islam in its purest sense to Afghanistan fit their definition of jihad. The Afghanistan cause became an overriding priority for militant Islamic fundamentalists from numerous Arab nations. They felt united by Islam, not national boundaries, and large numbers of these holy warriors were willing to go to Afghanistan to risk their lives for their religious beliefs. Osama bin Laden, who now fully supported the concept of Muslim solidarity, was among them.

# On to Afghanistan

COMING TO THE AID OF AFGHANISTAN gave Osama bin Laden a means of channeling his religious fervor. "I was enraged and went there at once," he said in describing his immediate reaction to the situation.[1] In many ways, this marked an important turning point in the young man's life. Instead of remaining at home and working in the family business, he had begun to strike off on a different path. Clearly, his decision was based on genuine religious zeal, yet early on it had been obvious that he was never going to be the star of the family business. Though highly intelligent and intuitive, Osama was just one of many bin Laden sons and he frequently became lost in the shuffle. A guest at the bin Laden company headquarters described how Osama was treated by his older half brother Salim:

[Mohammed] bin Laden's eldest son Salim, was my host at the family's lavish offices. Clean shaven and soft spoken, Osama was dressed in a well tailored Western suit and tie. There was no mistaking the unease with which Osama regarded his elder half brother. After our brief introduction, Salim dismissed Osama with a wave of his hand, and the young man backed off with a look of frustration in his eyes.[2]

After Mohammed bin Laden's death, all the children inherited large sums of money. Estimates of Osama's share vary from $60 million to over $330 million. Salim assumed the company's reins of power and when he unexpectedly died in a 1988 plane crash, another brother, named Baki, headed the dynasty. There would have always been a place for Osama in the family business but going to Afghanistan set his life on a different course.

Despite his eagerness to fight for Islam, bin Laden did not unthinkingly rush off to Afghanistan with a

*A vendor attempts to sell used stereo equipment in Afghanistan in March 2000. This equipment, along with other items and most forms of art, was banned by the Taliban, the ruling group in Afghanistan, and so discarded by its owners.*

rifle in his hand. Instead, he began by using both his mind and his money to advance the cause he believed in. Bin Laden's first stop was Pakistan—a solidly Muslim nation bordering Afghanistan. There he set up a recruitment station of sorts to bring Muslims from various Arab nations to fight the Afghanistan holy war. It didn't take long to see that Osama bin Laden's business skills would be extremely useful in this situation. He organized training camps where the recruits learned the art of strategic warfare. His ample fortune allowed him to help finance these projects, and as a result of his efforts, thousands of Muslim fighters came to the aid of their Afghan brothers.

Bin Laden knew these underground Islamic fighters would not last without a substantial support network. Therefore to ensure the movement's survival, he selectively recruited physicians, bomb experts, military strategists, and engineers from throughout the Arab world to aid the fighters. He even brought in Muslim experts in various fields from the United States and Western Europe.

Being in the building industry was a major plus in allowing bin Laden to construct the infrastructure necessary to win against the Soviets. Bulldozers, along with an assortment of other construction vehicles, soon arrived so that trenches could be dug and roads paved, permitting supplies to be brought in and forces moved to strategic areas. Under Osama bin Laden's direction, men who had come to fight the enemy did so in ways they hadn't anticipated. He quickly put them to work on construction crews so that the resistance would have stock depots, hospitals, and additional training sites.

It's been estimated that over 25,000 Muslim fighters from at least thirty-five countries participated in the Afghanistan struggle. These included a number of leaders from Islamic organizations already suspected of having terrorist connections. Among them was Islamic fundamentalist Dr. Ayman al-Zawahiri, a formerly high-ranking officer in the Egyptian intelligence service who at one point had been arrested for subversive activities in his country. Ayman al-Zawahiri and others like him forged lasting alliances with bin Laden, which continued long after the Soviets left Afghanistan in 1989. In their ongoing jihad, Ayman al-Zawahiri would later be considered one of bin Laden's top men.

During the 1980s, Afghanistan and nearby parts of Pakistan served as an invaluable gathering point and springboard for what many people would one day perceive as a worldwide terrorist movement. In fact, throughout this period, many of the newly arrived jihad fighters had needed special travel documents or false passports to get there. Already wanted in their own nations for subversive or terrorist activities, they had to travel under assumed identities.

Bin Laden, with his organizational skills and ample bank accounts, played an important role in drawing militant Islamic fundamentalists to Afghanistan. For them there was far more at stake than merely driving out the Soviets. These volunteers were there for the glory of Islam and they hoped to create a true Islamic nation. As Iranian analyst Amir Taheri described the jihadists' ultimate goal:

> The Afghan resistance movement has not confined itself to a minimum program of securing the nation's independence and territorial integrity, but openly advocates the creation of an Islamic society. It is in the name of Allah, and not of nationalism in the Western meaning of the term, that Soviet troops are gunned down in the mountains of Afghanistan. In some of the liberated zones the resistance movement has already brought into existence its ideal Islamic society. Here women have been pushed back into their veil, polygamy has been legalized, girls are kept out of school and the mullahs and muwlavis [religious leaders] exercise their tyrannical power in all spheres of life.[3]

Though support for the Afghanistan jihad came from Muslim countries and organizations, a key amount of assistance was also from what would seem a most unlikely place—the United States. In this instance, the old saying, "My enemy's enemy is my friend" applies.

The United States had been at odds with the Soviet Union for some time. It was anxious to stop Soviet expansion and the spread of communism in any way possible. By funding the Afghanistan rebels, the United States believed it was supporting a true struggle for freedom. The jihadists accepted U.S. backing—it meant money, weapons, and supplies. They made certain, however, to remain in full control of the operation. Anxious to separate the United States from the grassroots level of the struggle, rebel leaders kept U.S. representatives out of the training camps and away from their pivotal planning and strategy sessions.

At times a great deal of effort went into ensuring that the United States and Afghanistan's *mujahideen*, or holy fighters, remained at arms' length from one another. One Islamic intelligence officer noted that "no American or Chinese [China was another foe of the Soviet Union] instructor was ever involved in giving training on any kind of weapon or equipment to the mujahideen . . . This was a deliberate, carefully considered policy that we steadfastly refused to change despite mounting pressure from the CIA, and later from the U.S. Defense Department, to allow them to take over."[4]

According to at least one source, it was Osama bin Laden's idea to have the United States supply the fighters with Stingers, which are heat-seeking ground-to-air missiles with the capacity to bring down a Soviet fighter plane. Throughout the conflict, President

Ronald Reagan sent dozens of these weapons to Afghanistan along with training instructions for their most effective use. The Stingers enabled the Afghanistan fighters to down over 270 Soviet aircraft. Bin Laden was especially fond of this weapon. The U.S. State Department's file detailing bin Laden's background and activities even contains a 1986 photograph of him posing with a Stinger resting on his shoulder. It now seems unimaginable that we could be arming an Islamic extremist who a few years later would declare war on the United States.

Later on there were other unsettling revelations as well. Apparently some of the U.S. dollars sent for Afghanistan's war with the Soviet Union were funneled off for other purposes. Jihadist leaders sent the funds to extremist Islamic parties in Pakistan and other parts of the Muslim world. While the United States knew this was occurring to some extent, curbing Soviet expansion was considered such an important goal that U.S. officials chose to look the other way.

Osama bin Laden had no illusions about the United States' real objective in supporting the Afghan rebels. He later described it this way:

> The United States was not interested in our jihad. It was only afraid that Russia [the Soviet Union] would gain access to warm waters [a strategic spot in the Middle East]. The United States helped the mujahideen in order to con-

tain Russia. The mujahideen started their resistance much earlier. As soon as [former Soviet President] Gorbachev announced the withdrawal of Russian forces from Afghanistan, the United States . . . stopped [its] assistance for [the] mujahideen.[5]

Islamic extremists coming to Afghanistan's aid also received money from another somewhat unlikely source—Saudi Arabia's ruling family. Although Saudi royals claimed to be devout Muslims, they had often been criticized by Islamic fundamentalists for being too secular and too close to the West. As these Islamic extremists tended to be a disruptive element in Saudi society, Saudi leaders were pleased to see them focus their time and energy on the conflict in Afghanistan. It meant less pressure at home, which was something the Saudi regime was grateful for.

Since these groups were overtly hostile to the Saudi establishment, it would have been awkward to openly fund their cause, even if it meant getting them out of the way for a while. Instead, the money was quietly channeled through Osama bin Laden.

Bin Laden was in a unique position to be helpful here. Due to his father's close business and personal relationship with Saudi rulers, Osama had remained close to them despite his new affiliation with the extremists. Bin Laden saw to it that the cash was used to establish still more training camps in Afghanistan and nearby Pakistan. The royals were not aware that these camps not only trained Muslim youths for the Afghan struggle, but played a crucial role in indoctrinating the fighters who would later be internationally regarded as making up a network of Islamic terrorists. Volunteers there learned various methods of sabotage, including how to make bombs with sophisticated plastic explosives and remote-control detonators. They were also continuously drilled in Islamic teachings to reinforce their spiritual commitment to jihad.

Osama bin Laden did more than bring money and organizational skills to the war in Afghanistan, however. He also bravely fought on the battlefield alongside the other jihadists. As Hamza Mohammed, a Palestinian who'd come to Afghanistan to help drive out the Soviets, described bin Laden, "He was a hero to us because he was on the front line, always moving ahead of everybody else. He not only gave his money, but he also gave himself. He came down from his palace to live with the Afghan peasants and the Arab fighters. He cooked with them, ate with them, dug trenches with them. That was bin Laden's way."[6]

Early on, Osama bin Laden had made it clear that he wanted to do his part on the battlefield and did not wish to be treated like a celebrity. He thought of the predicament in Afghanistan as largely being that of Muslims "in a medieval society besieged by a twentieth century superpower." He was not afraid of death and is quoted as saying, "In our religion, there is a special place in the hereafter for those who participate in jihad. One day of [fighting] in Afghanistan was like a thousand days of praying in an ordinary mosque."[7] Radical Islamists, like bin Laden, were prepared to die for Allah if necessary. Through such actions they believed they would become martyrs to their cause.

Although there were many inspiring tales about bin Laden's bravery in the field, there are other less flattering stories about him as well. Some claim that at times Osama bin Laden's overzealousness actually interfered with a more effective approach to developing strategy. Supposedly bin Laden's areas of influence were strongest in certain parts of Afghanistan. When he would try to exert his influence in regions where others were in command, he was sometimes viewed as arrogant and extremely overbearing.

John Simpson, the World Affairs editor at the British Broadcasting Company (BBC), recalled one harrowing incident in which he was grateful bin Laden's instructions were ignored:

> I was filming a group of mujahideen in Afghanistan as they fired mortars at the nearby town of Jalalabad. An impressive-looking Arab in a beard and white robes [bin Laden], one of the many fundamentalist volunteers fighting alongside the mujahideen, suddenly appeared. Jumping up on the wall, he screamed that we were infidels [nonbe-

lievers in Islam] and that the mujahideen should kill us at once. They [the fighters in charge of the area] grinned and shrugged their shoulders, so he ran over to a truck driver and offered him $500 to run us down. The truck driver grinned too. Then the tall Arab ran off to the mujahideen sleeping quarters and there threw himself onto one of the beds, beating his fists on the pillow in frustration. My colleagues and I stood and watched him with a mixture of embarrassment and relief."[8]

There were other similar accounts of bin Laden's behavior. Yet for the most part, he was highly respected and undoubtedly a rising star in the Islamic fundamentalist movement.

The recruitment and training of volunteers for the Afghanistan jihad continued even after the Soviets agreed to withdraw and a cease-fire had been implemented. Although the Soviets left Afghanistan by February 1989, jihad recruitment was heaviest around that time. Many of the nearly 20,000 men who arrived then were among the most fanatical. These extremists were already deeply committed to establishing fundamentalist Islamic regimes in their homelands. Unlike the first holy fighters who'd come years before, these jihadists were less concerned about what was happening in Afghanistan than with being part of a much larger movement dedicated to fostering fundamental Islamic predominance throughout the Muslim world. They were also militantly anti-Western in every respect.

They would carry on the jihad in their own countries, which they regarded as corrupt and at odds with the true essence of Islam. Their acts of war would ultimately be felt in Algeria, Azerbaijan, Bangladesh, Bosnia, Tunisia, Sudan, Britain, and the United States, as well as in other places.

Theirs was a holy war that could be waged anywhere in the world that Islamic militants like Osama bin Laden deemed it necessary. In explaining the phenomenon, Benazir Bhutto, former prime minister of Pakistan, noted:

> It is all a consequence of the Afghan war, where a lot of indoctrination took place. [The Islamic fighters in Afghanistan] were told that if you have your faith you don't need anything else to demolish all the superpowers. They were brought up to believe you can demolish both the Soviet Union and the United States and all the world. And having driven the Soviet Union out of Afghanistan they feel they have the power to drive America out [of any Muslim land] as well.[9]

The realization that during the war in Afghanistan the United States had inadvertently helped to finance and develop a ripe Islamic terrorist training ground clearly proved to be an embarrassment for U.S. officials. The CIA calls these unanticipated occurrences "blowback," and following the Soviet withdrawal, more than one U.S. official painfully acknowledged that they were partly to blame for creating a new and dangerous enemy. Charles G. Cogan, a CIA operations chief, said at the time, "It's quite a shock. The hypothesis that the mujahideen would come to the United States and commit terrorist actions did not enter into our universe of thinking at the time. We were totally preoccupied with the war against the Soviets in Afghanistan. It was a significant unintended consequence."[10]

These sentiments were shared by Richard Murphy, former U.S. ambassador to Syria and Saudi Arabia who added, "We did spawn a monster in Afghanistan. Once the Soviets were gone [the Afghan rebels] were looking around for other targets and Mr. Osama bin Laden has settled on the United States as the source of all evil."[11]

Osama bin Laden's resentment of what he views as U.S. domination and interference in Muslim affairs was further heightened toward the end of the Afghanistan conflict. Convinced that the rebels needed one final push to drive the Soviet Union out, the United States and Saudi Arabia provided the money for a last massive offensive. The mujahideen were ultimately successful, but the offensive resulted in a tremendous death toll among the holy fighters. Bin Laden claimed that the United States was pleased to see this, since with the war winding down, America probably feared that the Islamic warriors were becoming too powerful. Bin Laden's rage over this incident further fueled his hatred of the West. He anxiously awaited the day when the United States would be forced to deal with an international Islamic army.

# 5

# Homecoming Hero

OSAMA BIN LADEN DID NOT BECOME an internationally wanted terrorist overnight. After the war in Afghanistan, however, things began to change for him. Following the Soviet withdrawal in 1989, he returned to Saudi Arabia in a new light. His experiences and relationships with the jihadists in Afghanistan had only increased his commitment to Islamic fundamentalism. What was truly different was how bin Laden was now viewed by others. Word of his bravery, leadership, and devotion to Islam had spread, making him a hero among his people.

*Osama bin Laden (right) is pictured in this image from Qatar's Al Jazeera TV at the wedding of one of his sons (left) in January 2001.*

Bin Laden's hero status had begun to grow even while he was in Afghanistan, and both the Saudi government and his family's business profited from his being in the limelight. By embracing a jihadist hero, Saudi rulers hoped to quell any further criticism from Islamic fundamentalists. Proud of the native son who had done so much for Islam, in 1983 King Fahd of Saudi Arabia awarded the bin Laden brothers what has been viewed as the most significant construction contract in Middle Eastern history. The corporation was paid $3 billion to restore the mosques at Mecca and Medina—the two holiest sites in the Islamic universe. It was also rumored that even though Osama was off fighting in Afghanistan at the time and not actually involved in the restoration project, he shared handsomely in the profits.

After the Afghanistan victory, bin Laden quickly rose to the role of returning hero. He spoke at mosques and other places, often drawing large crowds of young men who were soon inspired and anxious to help create an Islamic world. Frequently his stirring speeches were taped and it has been estimated that over a million of these tapes were sold or otherwise distributed throughout various Muslim countries. Many of bin Laden's tapes contain blatantly anti-American rhetoric. On one he shouted, "When we buy American goods, we are accomplices in the murder of Palestinians. American companies make millions in the Arab world with which they pay taxes to their government. The United States uses that money to send $3 billion a year to Israel which it uses to kill Palestinians."[1]

For a time Osama bin Laden continued to be embraced by the Saudi government. In fact, his entire family prospered as it was regularly awarded generous government construction contracts. Yet despite his sizable fortune, Osama bin Laden did not live the lavish lifestyle often associated with wealth. He moved into a modest apartment with his wife and children and tried to live according to strict Islamic teachings. There are those, however, who believed that Osama bin Laden would never simply lead a quiet religious existence. "Fire was raging within him," one family friend noted in describing the young man's disposition.[2] Others who knew him both in Afghanistan and at home felt similarly.

Regardless of his personality, bin Laden's life would dramatically change in August 1990 when Iraqi leader Saddam Hussein invaded the neighboring nation of Kuwait and seemed to be looking toward Saudi Arabia as his next target. Panic broke out among the Saudi royals as they feared they'd be unable to defend their country against an onslaught from Iraq.

Osama bin Laden immediately offered his assistance to the house of al-Saud. His experience in Afghanistan had enabled him to map out what he saw as an effective battle strategy for his country. Besides offering to enlist the Islamic jihadists he'd fought with in Afghanistan to supplement the Saudi army, bin Laden strongly urged that Saudi construction companies immediately be put to work building reinforcement areas and fortifications.

As he reminded Saudi leaders of their success in Afghanistan, bin Laden was passionate about saving the country using Muslim forces, and fiercely opposed to calling on the West (especially the United States) for assistance. He stressed that bringing in these foreign and corrupt influences would be contrary to Islamic teachings and would demoralize the nation. Bin Laden further warned the house of al-Saud that intervention by U.S. troops would make it extremely difficult for Islamic fundamentalists to support the Saudi government in the future.

To Islamic fundamentalists, involving the imperialist West in a conflict where Muslims were pitted against Muslims was sacrilegious. According to one source, bin Laden hurriedly barged into the office of Prince Sultan, Saudi Arabia's minister of defense, with a ten-page alternative battle plan. Furious, bin Laden shouted, "There is no need for American troops!" But he didn't have a solid answer for the prince when asked how the country would adequately defend itself against an air or naval attack from Saddam Hussein. Prince Sultan had also further inquired, "What do you plan to do about Iraq's chemical and biological weapons?" Bin Laden's only reply was, "We will defeat them with our faith."[3]

U.S. forces arrived shortly thereafter. Believing their survival as an independent nation was at stake, Saudi Arabia invited the West. The result was the Gulf War, in which the United States led a group of Western European nations in a stinging assault on Iraq. At least for a time, Saddam Hussein was pushed back. But to the outrage of Islamic fundamentalists, U.S. military forces remained poised in the region in case Hussein again posed a threat.

Despite their decision, at first Osama bin Laden appeared to remain loyal to the Saudi leadership. Other Islamic fundamentalists wholeheartedly condemned the house of al-Saud, but bin Laden initially viewed the U.S. intrusion as the Saudi government's panic response. He felt the nation could be restored to its Islamic roots if the foreign troops speedily withdrew once the immediate crisis was over.

However, Saudi leaders knew full well that wasn't going to happen, and while Osama bin Laden's hero status and popularity with the masses formerly benefited them, they were aware that now it could work against them. Believing that bin Laden was sufficiently powerful to sway public sentiment negatively, the house of al-Saud warned him not to openly condemn its actions. To further intimidate the national hero, they threatened to withdraw the lucrative government building contracts his family's business had long enjoyed.

Before long Osama bin Laden's relationship with the house of al-Saud deteriorated to the point at which he felt it was wise to leave the country. Obviously the sentiment was mutual. Linking him to antigovernment plots, Saudi Arabia expelled bin Laden in 1991. Three years later in 1994, it would even revoke his citizenship.

Osama bin Laden fled to Sudan—a country with a government in accord with Islamic fundamentalism. He arrived there with his immediate family, which by then had grown considerably. Now in his thirties, Osama bin Laden had three wives. Besides his Syrian wife, he had married two women from Saudi Arabia. Osama grew up in a large family and produced one of his own as well. Between his wives, there were fifteen children with his eldest sons Mohammed, Omar, and Saad being his favorites. After arriving in Sudan, the entire family moved into a brick and stucco home in Khartoum—a city where militant Islamic fundamentalists from numerous countries had taken refuge.

Bin Laden also purchased a second home on the banks of the Blue Nile, where he relaxed on weekends with his wives and children. Both these dwellings were extremely modest—not at all like the palatial homes of his extended family still residing in Saudi Arabia. Despite temperatures during the day of over 100 degrees, bin Laden decided against installing air-conditioning in either house. It was not uncommon for him to shun luxuries that he could easily afford. At least one journalist quoted him as saying, "I don't want to get used to the good life."[4]

Osama bin Laden purposely avoided the excesses of affluent living and refused to expose his family to needless waste. Instead, the bin Ladens lived a simple and deeply religious life. Osama's wives were well versed in the Koran and they instructed other women in it at a nearby mosque. As for bin Laden, part of being true to Islam meant waging jihad and that would eventually come to mean an involvement in international terrorism.

His break with Saudi Arabia ended Osama bin Laden's involvement in the lucrative construction industry. Essentially a skilled businessman, bin Laden decided to go into the import-export business while living in Sudan. He began establishing relationships with various financial institutions in countries sympathetic to Islamic fundamentalism. Perhaps not by chance, these connections would prove useful later on for more sinister purposes.

The atmosphere in Sudan was ripe for someone like bin Laden to find support for his ideology as well as ways to put these ideas into action. The Gulf War and the continued presence of U.S. forces in the Middle East had severely shaken the sensibilities of Islamic fundamentalists in the region. More than ever before, they viewed Muslim nations that welcomed the U.S. presence in the Persian Gulf as mere props of the imperialist West. Fundamentalist groups now believed that it would soon be necessary to overthrow these regimes in order to establish true Islamic states.

To achieve their goal these militants planned to strike at U.S. targets throughout the world. It was their hope that a relentless terrorist campaign would ultimately force the United States to withdraw permanently from the Middle East. Without the support of the United States, the more secular governments in the region could be toppled and replaced with Islamic fundamentalist regimes. A good deal of the planning and implementation of this scheme rested with a group Osama bin Laden had had a key role in developing. It was known as al Qaeda.

Many al Qaeda members were comfortable with as well as schooled in various terrorist methods. A good number of these young men had been jihadists in Afghanistan. Following the Gulf War, increasing numbers of these holy fighters and others like them had been sent by Islamic fundamentalist leaders to various parts of the world where there were sizable Muslim populations. The jihadists' mission was to incite Islamic revolution and carry out acts of terrorism against the enemy. Today active cells (small groups) of these mujahideen exist in pockets of Europe, Africa, Asia, and even the United States. There are secret training bases and reinforcement networks in nations sympathetic to their cause including Afghanistan, Pakistan, Iran, and Sudan. Al Qaeda was made up of a number of terrorist divisions. The various divisions were concerned with religion, the media, finance, and military operations.

Much of bin Laden's further involvement with terrorist groups stemmed from his relationship with Hassan Abdallah al-Turabi, the Islamic spiritual leader of Sudan. In many ways bin Laden became a favorite of the religious leader. Turabi worked with bin Laden on enhancing his spiritual development, while bin Laden assisted with Turabi's plans for a far-reaching Islamic revolution. Bin Laden generously gave of his time and skill to help foster the growth of Turabi's jihadist group, the Popular International Organization (PIO). Turabi had defined the group's mission "to work out a global action plan in order to challenge and defy the tyrannical West, because Allah can no longer remain in our world, in the face of the absolute materialistic power."[5]

At times bin Laden's business and financial expertise helped keep the growing terrorist network afloat. It was more than the substantial amount of money he'd left Saudi Arabia with. Bin Laden also had connections with various international financial institutions (some more scrupulous than others) and could use his own accounts and business dealings to channel money for terrorist purposes to wherever it needed to go. To this end he established a string of accounts in banks throughout the Middle East, Europe, and Asia, which combined his own funds along with those of other wealthy Islamic businessmen supporting the Islamic revolution.

Working with extremely affluent Islamics, as he had in the Afghanistan war, bin Laden helped Turabi by establishing the Shamal (North) Islamic Bank. The sole purpose of this newly formed financial institution was to fund radical Islamic terrorism. It is estimated that bin Laden supplied the bank with nearly $50 million of his own money. In return for his assistance, Sudan's government supposedly gave him over a million acres of Sudanese land, which he used for farming and cattle raising.

Osama bin Laden was also the mastermind behind an entirely separate financial entity known as the Brotherhood Group. Through this effort, more than 125 of the wealthiest pro-Islamic men in the Middle East were given a discreet way to generously support terrorism. Bin Laden's goal was to hide terrorist funding sources from Western surveillance operations, and he effectively used the legitimate business assets of a number of these men to do so.

Since many members of the Brotherhood Group owned large companies in the United States, bin Laden was also able to smuggle terrorists into America by arranging for them to be company employees. This disguised their true purpose for being there as well as allowed them to inconspicuously enter and remain in the United States on legal business visas. Bin Laden had the same arrangement with a significant number of Brotherhood Group members who owned companies throughout much of Europe.

Though unable to either directly trace or stop the financial flow, in 1994 Egyptian intelligence sources were aware that the amounts of cash being siphoned off for terrorist purposes were extremely high. In describing the Brotherhood Group's operation it was noted that "the money is used for buying weapons and explosives, [and] paying the salaries of executors of terrorist operations."[6]

Bin Laden engineered ways to amply support Islamic terrorists in Bosnia-Herzegovina (the former Yugoslavia) as well. In this money scheme he channeled funds to between four and six thousand terrorists through various Islamic charities that were of questionable legitimacy. There were similar bin Laden-sponsored charities in other areas of the world. Naturally, some of the money did go to the destitute and sick and such aid helped build the support base necessary for a future Islamic revolution as well as kept the operations somewhat legitimate.

Besides setting up a crucial financial network for the Islamic revolution during the early 1990s, Osama bin Laden aided the cause in a second vital way. He put the skills he had learned in the construction industry to work to enhance the spread of terrorism by establishing the building company known as the al-Hijrah for Construction and Development, Ltd. The sole purpose of this construction enterprise was to build an infrastructure in Sudan to move the equipment, vehicles, and weaponry needed to expedite terrorist acts. Roads linking cities, seaports, and terrorist training bases were constructed. A modern airport large enough to accommodate combat aircraft went up as well.

Bin Laden's many contributions to the Islamic revolution earned him the trust and respect of the movement's highest leaders. There was no doubt that Osama bin Laden had made a difference in ways that would please Islamic militants and eventually frighten the West. A report by Human Rights Watch, a division of Amnesty International, stated that bin Laden "was able to establish a powerful military and political presence in Sudan." The report further noted that the Islamic fighters amassing there included "Tunisians, Algerians, Sudanese, Saudis, Syrians, Iraqis, Moroccans, Somalis, Ethiopians, Eritreans, Chechnyans, Bosnians and six African Americans."[7] Bin Laden was obviously capable of helping to put together a sizable terrorist force. Thanks to his work and that of others like him, by the mid-1990s the Islamic terrorist network had been significantly enlarged and enhanced.

Though he was frequently praised, Osama bin Laden was not a person who thrived on adoration and often preferred to remain in the background. He was very much of a team player, content to do whatever he could for the cause that was now at the center of his life. Yet he would not be able to stay in the background for long. Bin Laden was rapidly rising up the hierarchy and was well on his way to becoming one of the Islamic revolution's elite.

# Moving
# Up

MANY YOUNG MUSLIM MEN CONTINUED to be drawn into the growing army of Islamic revolutionaries. After joining they would be trained by hard-core members of this group—the men who had fought in Afghanistan and were frequently referred to as "Afghans." All Islamic revolutionaries learned to use automatic weapons, but they also needed to know how to conduct guerrilla warfare effectively. One Arab observer described the Afghans and their newer recruits as "the military arm of a number of Islamic movements and operations in certain Arab and Muslim countries."[1]

To overthrow the Western-controlled governments and establish Islamic regimes in Muslim countries, they would have to come up against well-armed conventional armies. That meant the Islamic militants

needed to fight in unconventional ways. They would have to strike and disappear. They would have to leave their enemy shocked, dazed, and wondering how to retaliate against an opponent they couldn't find.

In describing their style, one Arab official said of the Islamic fundamentalist fighters, "[They] attack, sow violence, and assassinate such 'state symbols' as government officials, policemen, security agents, and the military in Algeria and Egypt. They detonate bombs and strike state institutions and buildings."[2]

To accomplish this, the fighters were trained in the use of weapons that could be readily concealed, as well as in various aspects of bomb making. They also learned how to infiltrate numerous legitimate groups and falsify documents to place themselves where they needed to be.

These new fighters greatly admired bin Laden. By now his reputation had grown internationally and incoming militants were well aware of all he had done for the cause. Many idolized him and dreamed of being just like him. However, it's doubtful that they could have been. It had taken more than religious fervor and battle bravery to get bin Laden where he had risen to in the movement. Osama bin Laden was an extremely

*Exploiting brutal unrest and famine in Somalia, bin Laden sought to establish jihad, or holy war, in that country in an effort to expel Western influence.*

intelligent and well-educated individual with out-standing financial and organizational skills. While many of the fighters entering the ranks showed promise, others fell far short of this ideal.

Following his capture, one terrorist described the men who followed bin Laden as: "People who had no success in life, had nothing in their heads and wanted to join just to keep from falling on their noses . . . people who loved their religion but had no idea what their religion really meant, [and people with] nothing in their heads but to fight and solve all the problems in the world with battles."[3] Yet even though the jihadists were hardly an elite fighting force, there were some intelligent, well-directed men within the ranks and Osama bin Laden would come to use their talents to best achieve his aims.

In the fall of 1992 while bin Laden resided in Sudan, the Islamic revolution set its sights on sub-Saharan Africa. Turabi had long hoped to spread Islamic fundamentalism in Africa and bin Laden was prepared to do whatever was necessary to assist him. He began by setting up a string of businesses in several East African nations. These would afford the revolutionaries cash as well as establish a legitimate presence in these areas.

The overall idea, as always, was to foment political unrest and destabilize the existing governments to establish Islamic regimes eventually. The militants took on the challenge, often using educational meetings and charity work to begin to sway the population toward Islamic fundamentalism. The effects of their efforts were soon apparent as there was a notable increase in riots in both Kenya and Uganda. Somalia, Tanzania, and Chad were other targets.

A second goal of the Islamic radicals was to rid the area known as the Horn of Africa of any remnant of U.S. presence or Western influence. The Horn of Africa, which includes the nations of Ethiopia, Eritrea, Somalia, and Djibouti, has long been considered a strategically important region because of its geographical position. Located on the eastern tip of Africa, it is vital to international shipping, since it is here that the Red Sea connects with the Indian Ocean. If strategic access points along Somalia's coast were blocked off, ships would be unable to reach the Suez Canal. This would disrupt shipping traffic between Europe and the United States as well as between Europe and East Asia, and in some instances, the effect on commerce would be devastating.

Even before Islamic fundamentalists set their sights on it, the Horn of Africa had been a point of political and social unrest. There were religious rivalries between Muslims and Christians, and tensions stemming from ethnic and tribal affiliations further threatened to undermine the existing governments.

Located on the Horn of Africa, Somalia had never been a strong united country. In 1992 fierce fighting broke out between clans as each fought to maintain its identity and independence. The brutal ongoing warfare resulted in a great deal of bloodshed and devastation. The situation was worsened by a severe drought that had resulted in widespread famine throughout much of the nation.

Americans were moved by pictures of starving Somalian children on television, and in 1992 the United States pledged humanitarian aid to the innocent victims who were often cut off from the little available food by the feuding factions. In December of that year, United States, along with UN troops, arrived on the scene with both food and medical supplies. They were not there to intervene in the conflict but to feed the starving victims of the country's homegrown strife. It was to be a strictly humanitarian mission and had been appropriately named Operation Restore Hope.

Yet the food deliverers were mostly soldiers, and neither side in the conflict wanted them there. At times each of the major factions involved in Somalia's civil strife feared that Western intervention could shift the balance of power against them. Also, the warring sides often tried to use the famine to their advantage. By physically cutting off certain segments of the population from an ongoing food supply, they effectively eliminated pockets of the enemy's support base.

During the conflict, the Islamic fundamentalists had heightened their charitable work, and as might be expected, they were virulently against the proposed humanitarian intervention by the West. One Islamic group known as the World Muslim Relief Organization claimed that "only Muslim organizations have been doing [true] humane work in Somalia."[4] It further asserted that the West's offer to help was really "a suspicious plan aimed at partitioning Somalia to European countries and of implementing the partition plan by fanning the flames of dissension among Somali factions fighting for government control."[5] It's significant to note that the World Muslim Relief Organization was part of a broader network of associations that for the most part had been organized by Osama bin Laden.

Not surprisingly, not all the money the Islamic fundamentalists poured into Somalia went for charitable purposes. The fundamentalists themselves took advantage of the already existing unrest in Somalia to further their own cause. Bin Laden used both his financial expertise and knowledge of the construction trade to ensure that actively functioning jihadist training bases were established there. These bases were used to train recruited Somalian soldiers for the Islamic revolution as well as serve as military installations. All were well stocked with an array of weaponry and armaments. In describing the type of instruction that was given at these camps, a defector later said, "[The recruits] receive rough training in all types of combat, violence, and assassinations . . ."[6] Bin Laden also had radio stations and various other communication systems installed in key parts of Somalia.

A flood of highly seasoned Islamic terrorists were sent into the area by Islamic fundamentalist leaders. Some operated from separate independent units, while others infiltrated both sides of the warring forces. The plan, as always, was to destabilize the existing governmental system and establish an Islamic regime. If the United States tried to enter the picture, it was equally essential to drive it from the country.

Many Islamic fundamentalists, including Osama bin Laden, believed that the United States was more interested in gaining a foothold in Somalia than in genuinely providing assistance to a hungry population. They warned that if the United States established itself in Somalia, its next target was likely to be Sudan. With control of Sudan, they argued, the United States would ensure that Islamic revolutionaries would never control the geographically strategic Horn of Africa. Hizballah, an Islamic group reportedly engaged in terrorist activities, noted:

> The [U.S.] return to the Horn of Africa is intended to confront the Islamic revival that shines from the Horn of Africa. This is not the first intervention and will not be the last. Washington must throw its weight and military strength against every Islamic or national awakening in any area that seeks to achieve independence and end subservient policies.

This will be a common phenomenon by the
end of this century and into the next.[7]

The armed Islamic movement in Somalia was growing
fast and preparing itself for the challenge. To jihadists
like Osama bin Laden, it was a matter of looking out
for Islamic interests on an international scope.

Meanwhile, in Somalia, Islamic forces readied
themselves for guerrilla attacks against the United
States. The fundamentalists also did their best to incite
the local population. As one observer recalled,
"Hostility toward a UN presence is manifested in
Friday sermons in Somalia's mosques."[8] An attack
against U.S. targets in Aden, Yemen, where preparations for the humanitarian aid to Somalia were
underway, was planned as well. Since Osama bin Laden
had extensive connections with former Afghanistan
fighters now positioned in Yemen, he was selected as
the project's coordinator.

A team of about five hundred skilled terrorists was
summoned to the area as funds to support the operation were speedily funneled to bin Laden's Yemen
business accounts. Expert bomb makers had been
called in and the necessary materials gathered. Sheik
Tariq al-Fadi, who had been in exile in London, arrived
to help with the preparations and organize the fighters.

Bin Laden didn't have much time to plan the strike
but he still managed to inflict a substantial amount of

damage. Just four days after Christmas two hotels in Aden—the Aden Hotel and the Golden Moor—were bombed. Both hotels were frequently used by U.S. military personnel in the area. Three people were killed and five more were wounded in the attack. A second part of the plan was foiled when a group of Islamic terrorists were apprehended just outside Aden airport. They had come equipped with RPG-7 rocket launchers, intending to target U.S. Air Force transport planes. Sheik Tariq al-Fadi and his helpers eventually gave themselves up to the police. This was done so that authorities could "solve" the crime and hopefully not look further for the kingpins like Osama bin Laden who had masterminded the undertaking.

Yet it would not be that easy to hide bin Laden's extensive involvement in terrorist activities. As Egyptian intelligence concluded after it had been called in by Yemen's government to assist in the investigation, "The leader of the terrorist groups that are trying to spoil security and stability in Yemen is a person named Osama bin Laden."[9]

Bin Laden's terrorist career was just beginning. He continued to be useful as large numbers of Islamic terrorists were moved from various parts of the world to Sudan, which had become his operations base. These included separate and distinct Islamic fighting units that had agreed to work together to force the UN and U.S. forces out of Somalia. Among them were Lebanese Hizballah fighters and members of Sudan's Islamic

Front. Many of the men recruited for Somalia were said to have "specialized in gang wars, street fighting, booby-trapped cars, commando operations and sniping operations."[10]

The overall idea was "to confront the Americans in Somalia" with the goal of "drawing them into a land war, street battles, attack and retract, and ambushes, as was done in Vietnam."[11] The combat center was to be the Somali city of Mogadishu, and as the United States retreated to what they would perceive to be safer rural areas, other Islamic forces would be waiting to strike them there.

Islamic fundamentalists saw the Somali operation as a segment in "a plan to expand the battle into other areas of the Horn of Africa, and to be a broad armed mass mobilization against America and the West . . . in . . . a grand war of vengeance between Islamists and the United States, whose outcome would be even worse than the result of the Vietnam War."[12]

Osama bin Laden was a pivotal figure in setting up the camps and training bases for the fighters headed for the Mogadishu offensive. It was his job to coordinate weapons, food, lodging, medical care, and transportation for a fighting force of thousands. In many cases these troops had to be inconspicuously moved through several countries to reach Somalia undetected. Frequently they were forced to travel through large tracts of desert to reach their ultimate destination. As was frequently his role, Osama bin Laden was also counted on to manipulate the international funding sources to provide sufficient cash for these maneuvers.

Attacks on U.S. and UN troops as well as on civilian rescue workers were carried out in both Mogadishu and other parts of Somalia during the summer of 1993. Local Somalis were urged to take up arms and support the militant Islamic fighters through leaflets and continuous propaganda broadcasts over Islamic radio stations. Noted Islamic fundamentalist writer Farah al Mohammad Duurgube declared, "Somalia fighters have agreed to defend their country, the dignity of their people, and their religion, and to make the neo-colonialist taste hell on earth. God willing, in the here-after they [the Americans] will also be cast into hell even worse than that [Mogadishu]. Let us kill them all, right to the last of these demoralized colonists."[13]

U.S. retaliation for these attacks only fueled the militant Islamic propaganda machine and the fighting continued into the fall. In addition to his other contributions, Osama bin Laden played an important part in the Islamic fundamentalist struggle in Somalia serving as an on-site field commander. His role was far more crucial than that of even the most skilled bomb maker or sharpshooter. The guerrilla campaign could not have sustained itself without the continuous replenishment of weapons and supplies, and bin Laden made certain that these resources were always on hand.

At various times during the fighting, it was up to bin Laden to see that well-known terrorists with highly specialized skills were brought in from other areas. This was not an easy task, since many of the men he wanted were also wanted by the authorities. But bin Laden had a reputation for being able to smuggle anything into a country and he fully lived up to it in this case. At times, men and weapons were hidden in traveling caravans carrying various goods through the desert. Bin Laden also hired a fleet of fishing boats to smuggle men as well as artillery from neighboring countries into Somalia. He even recruited experienced pilots who had flown in supplies to Afghanistan. Now in Somalia these men managed to land small cargo planes carrying sophisticated weaponry on makeshift airstrips in the dead of night. Those around him quickly saw that Osama bin Laden was a man who could make things happen.

Whenever necessary, bin Laden used his own funds to supplement the money available from other sources. It is believed that in numerous instances the jihadists would not have been nearly as successful without bin Laden's personal resources. One London scholar described the effect of bin Laden's funding on the movement as follows: "There was a time when people thought that any support for international terrorism must be state-centered [sponsored by a sympathetic country]. The bin Laden phenomenon is an illustration of the privatization of the support of terrorism."[14]

Meanwhile U.S. and UN forces were dismayed over what their humanitarian aid mission had become. On October 3, 1993, U.S. troops engaged in the fighting suffered heavy casualties. Eighteen American soldiers were killed and many more were wounded. To celebrate their victory, Islamic fundamentalists dragged the bodies of several American servicemen through the streets the following day. It would later be learned that the men engaged in much of that fighting had been "trained by al Qaeda [bin Laden's group]."[15]

Osama bin Laden would later speak proudly of the jihadists' role in the Somalia victory, noting:

> It is true that my companions fought . . . against the U.S. troops in Somalia. But we are fighting against U.S. terrorism. Under the cover of [the] United Nations, the United States tried to establish its bases in Somalia so that it could get control over Sudan and Yemen. My associates killed the Americans. . . . We are not ashamed of our jihad. In one explosion one hundred Americans were killed, then eighteen more were killed fighting. One day our men shot down an American helicopter. The pilot got out. We caught him, tied his legs and dragged him through the streets. After that 28,000 U.S. soldiers fled Somalia. The Americans are cowards.[16]

Though Osama bin Laden has been known to inflate casualty figures as well as dramatize events, U.S. forces did begin to pull out of Somalia soon after the October 3 incident. By the spring of the following year, only a smattering of American troops were left. In years to come, Osama bin Laden would refer to the Islamic offensive in Somalia as an important juncture in his development as a jihadist. His role in procuring fighters and supplies had made it all possible. Personally, he had gained valuable experience in decision and policy making on a broader level than he previously had. He also established relationships with jihadist organizations and Islamic intelligence services that would aid him in future jihadist ventures.

Bin Laden counted the withdrawal of U.S. troops from Mogadishu as among his most significant victories against America. Following it he reasoned that if it were possible to drive the United States out of Somalia, it was possible to purge the entire Middle East of Western influences. He would later express his feelings to a reporter this way:

> We believe that God used our holy war in Afghanistan to destroy the Russian army and the Soviet Union . . . and now we ask God to use us one more time to do the same to the Americans to make it [the U.S.] a shadow of itself. We also believe our war against the United States is much simpler than our war

against the Soviet Union, because some of our mujahideen who fought here in Afghanistan also participated in operations against the Americans in Somalia—and they were surprised at the collapse of American morale. This convinced us that the Americans are a paper tiger.[17]

On a broader scale the Islamic fundamentalists were now certain that the operational networks bin Laden and others had developed in East Africa and the Persian Gulf area were functional. Their participation in Mogadishu allowed them to see which strategies and maneuvers worked particularly well and they felt sure that this knowledge would be useful in future anti-American campaigns. The experience had boosted Osama bin Laden's confidence and he felt especially ready to take on the United States in a larger arena. In some instances, that would mean planning strikes in areas where the United States had special interests or even choosing targets closer to his enemy's home.

# Expanding
# Operations

PRIOR TO THE FIGHTING IN SOMALIA, Western intelligence sources had known of Osama bin Laden, but he was not considered a serious threat. Now things had changed. Pleased with his performance in Somalia, Turabi, along with other Islamic fundamentalist leaders, arranged for bin Laden to become a substantially more powerful component in fomenting an international jihad. For his next assignment, Osama bin Laden was asked to set his sights on Europe.

Osama would not disappoint his backers as he turned his attention toward bolstering the Islamic fundamentalist movement in the Balkans. War torn Bosnia-Herzegovina and Kosovo, where the oppression of Muslims had resulted in both discrimination and bloodshed, were ripe targets. Bin Laden began by

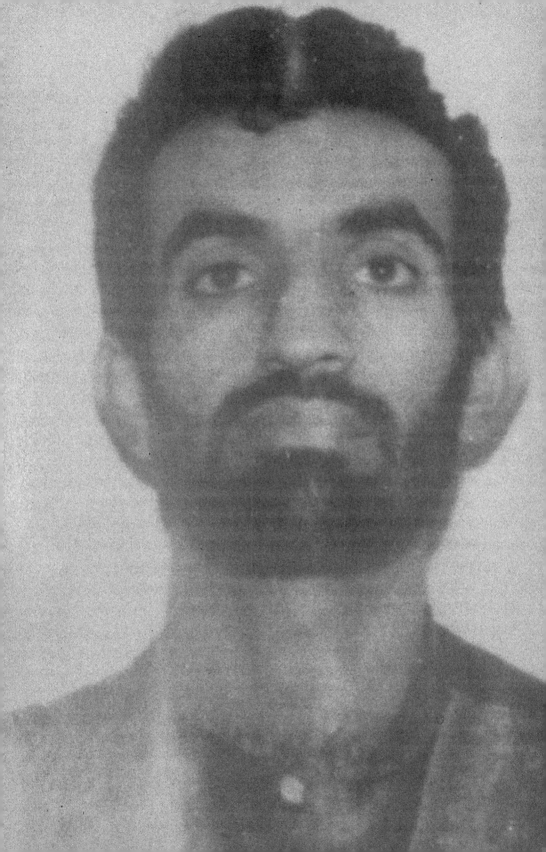

enlarging and enhancing his already substantial network of charitable and social-service agencies, which also served as fronts for clandestine terrorist activity.

While these were part of a broader terrorist network, bin Laden made sure that each outlet operated independently. That way if Western intelligence detected terrorist activity in one location, it could not be traced to the others. To further deflect the authorities, bin Laden would arbitrarily close these agencies and open new ones under different names. He also made a point of transferring personnel from region to region. The idea was to make things as confusing as possible for Western intelligence agents. Osama bin Laden also expanded the financial avenues he had established in Eastern Europe, ensuring that the jihadists had an adequate supply of cash at their disposal.

By 1994 the Islamic fundamentalists had decided to extend their network's reach to Western Europe and the United States. Osama bin Laden was called upon to assist in launching this venture as well. It was his responsibility to saturate Muslim communities in Europe and the United States with pro-Islamic/anti-Western propaganda. Bin Laden developed an effective

*Ramzi Ahmad Yousef, a valuable assistant to Osama bin Laden, was a major player in the 1993 bombing of the World Trade Center in New York City.*

format for the data and had it translated into numerous languages. The materials were distributed at various meetings and agencies. Bin Laden also relied heavily on the Internet and e-mail to get the word out. He proved to be quite adept at communications. Before long, the information network he created became global and remained in high gear for a number of years.

Bin Laden frequently went to Europe to expand his array of contacts as well as to oversee the trafficking of information. He stayed in England for a time and even purchased property in a London suburb. While there, he established several small organizations whose sole purpose was to find safe havens for Islamic militants hiding from the authorities.

By 1994, Osama bin Laden had become a wanted man himself and traveling to Europe as well as many other locations had become extremely dangerous for him. Due to his role in the terrorist activity in Somalia, the United States had pressured Saudi Arabia to take action against him. Therefore on April 7, 1994, the Saudi government revoked bin Laden's citizenship, citing that he had "committed acts that adversely affected the brotherly relations between the Kingdom of Saudi Arabia and some other countries."[1]

There was also a warrant out for his arrest. Bin Laden had gotten into England with his Saudi passport, which was no longer valid. The Saudi government knew he was there and had petitioned England to capture and return him. If he had been returned to Saudi

Arabia, it's likely that Osama bin Laden would have been swiftly executed.

For some time now, his activities had been extremely disruptive to the house of al-Saud's relationship with the West and Saudi Arabia had come to depend heavily on U.S. support. Some think that bin Laden stayed in England longer than it was safe for him to do so, but he was a man used to taking risks. The Islamic revolution had become a passion that ruled his life, and bin Laden put it ahead of any regard he may have had for his family or even his personal safety. Nevertheless, once he had accomplished his goals in Europe, bin Laden returned to his home in Sudan where he was shielded by an Islamic fundamentalist regime.

Bin Laden would not be home for long, though. Instead, he was about to expand his terrorist résumé to include directly overseeing a broad-based terrorist operation in the Pacific. Militant Islamic leaders who'd been impressed with bin Laden's organizational skills in supplying materials and disseminating information were now ready to have him plan and implement actual terrorist acts on a far broader scale. His new arena was to be the Philippines, where militant Islamics hoped to pit the Muslim community in the nation's southern islands against the Christians in the north.

Bin Laden began the task by arranging for small groups of terrorists to be relocated throughout the Philippines, often placed in large cities where they would be less likely to stand out. One of the people bin Laden arranged to have help him run the network was Ramzi Ahmad Yousef, a man with the dubious distinction of being a major player in the 1993 World Trade Center bombing in New York City. U.S. intelligence sources had been aware of an association between bin Laden and Ramzi Yousef after the Joint Terrorist Task Force found bin Laden's phone numbers among those listed on the phone company's record of calls Yousef and his accomplices made shortly before the bombing.

Despite concrete evidence to the contrary, however, when asked in an interview if he knew Yousef, bin Laden answered, "Ramzi Yousef, after the World Trade Center bombing became a well-known Muslim personality and all Muslims know him. Unfortunately, I did not know him before the incident." Bin Laden also had nothing but praise for Yousef, adding that he will always think of him "as a Muslim who defended Islam from American aggression. [Yousef] took this effort to let Americans know that their government assaults Muslims to ensure Israeli intent, to ensure Jews. America will see many youths who will follow Ramzi Yousef."[2]

In the Philippines, Yousef would serve as bin Laden's chief commander. Their goal was to expand and solidify regional terrorist operations. There's evidence that the group hoped to assassinate President Bill Clinton during his 1994 visit to the Philippines but that they were unable to breach U.S. security precautions. It was later learned that a plot to assassinate the pope in January 1995 while he was in Manila was only narrowly thwarted when the appointed bomb maker made an error that ruined the needed explosives.

Operating from the Philippines, the group had also planned to have two U.S. airplanes heading for Hong Kong from different directions simultaneously blow up in midair. This type of attack would become bin Laden's trademark. His later assaults increasingly revealed a fascination with highly synchronized, choreographed strikes. The two U.S. planes never blew up, but while working with bin Laden, Yousef managed to plant a bomb on a Philippine Airline (PAL) Boeing 747 flight that was headed for Tokyo. The bomb wasn't large enough to destroy the aircraft, but a Japanese traveler on board was killed.

After raiding a terrorist safe house in Manila, the police found evidence of extensive plans for additional terrorist attacks throughout the Philippines. These included U.S. targets there. There were also outlines for future attacks on the U.S. mainland. Some arrests were made, but many of bin Laden's group fled to safety in countries sympathetic to their cause.

Ramzi Yousef, however, was later apprehended in Pakistan and extradited to the United States to stand trial. He was convicted in September 1996 "of conspiracy to bomb U.S. airlines in Asia and in November

1997 for masterminding the Trade Center bombings."[3] At the time of his arrest he was hiding in an apartment complex owned by none other than Osama bin Laden. The connections were inescapable. U.S. intelligence sources kept finding ties to bin Laden in countries throughout the world. As his CIA file continued to grow, there was little doubt in the minds of authorities that bin Laden had become a major player in international terrorism.

There were a number of rumors about Osama bin Laden's personal life while he was in the Philippines. Some say that his fourth wife is a Muslim from the Philippines and that her brother assisted in bin Laden's terrorist schemes. Yet this has not been substantiated and it remains exceedingly difficult for authorities, or anyone else for that matter, to glean information regarding bin Laden's family affairs.

By 1995, Osama bin Laden turned his attention away from the Philippines and began to focus more on the Middle Eastern nations most responsible for the roadblocks to the establishment of Islamic fundamentalist regimes throughout the Muslim world. These were the countries that had invited in and embraced the West at what bin Laden believed was Islam's expense. Islamic fundamentalists had come to see both Egypt and Saudi Arabia as such enemies of their cause and they set about to treat these countries as enemies.

From an American perspective the idea of Muslims fighting Muslims in a religious war seems difficult to comprehend, but the rationale behind this was clearly established at the Islamic Religious Conference held in Sudan in April 1993. The conference issued a fatwa, or religious document, dealing with the matter. A fatwa is a decree issued by either an Islamic spiritual leader or Islamic court. Fatwas carry the weight of laws in fundamentalist communities and must be followed by all believers. The fatwa that came out of the 1993 conference made it clear that Muslims who fight against an Islamic state are not true Muslims and must be dealt with accordingly. It stated:

> Therefore the rebels who are Muslims and are fighting against the [Islamic] state are hereby declared Kaffir [infidels or nonbelievers] who have been standing up against the efforts of preaching, proselytization, and spreading Islam into Africa. However, Islam has justified the fighting and killing of both categories without any hesitation whatsoever with the following Koranic evidence . . .[4]

Those who aren't comfortable with the concept of Muslims killing Muslims for the sake of jihad are dealt with severely as well. As further noted in the fatwa: "Those Muslims who . . . try to question or doubt Islamic justifiability of jihad are hereby classified as 'hypocrites,' who are no longer Muslims, and also 'apostates' from the religion of Islam; and that they will be condemned permanently to the fire of Hell."[5]

The fatwa decreed in 1993 would open the door to an intensive campaign against Saudi Arabia and Egypt. Osama bin Laden's role in the Islamic revolutionary struggle had evolved through the years and with this undertaking would continue to do so. He would be a very vital player in organizing and implementing terrorist assaults against the land of his birth.

# 8

## Back Home

EVEN WHILE HE WAS IN SUDAN, LONDON, and the Philippines, Osama bin Laden remained a hero to the Islamic fundamentalists in Saudi Arabia. He was a homegrown fighter who had given up both a life of ease and his homeland for his beliefs. Osama bin Laden's story was especially inspiring to the large numbers of young men who had grown up hearing tales of his bravery in Afghanistan. Many hoped to be just like him and would carefully listen to every word of his taped speeches, which continued to be smuggled illegally into Saudi Arabia after his exile.

Though bin Laden saw the Islamic struggle as international in scope, he had a decidedly soft spot for the jihadists from Saudi Arabia. Through the years, he had kept in close touch with a number of groups there and

# MURDER

Nairobi & Dar es Salaam bombings, 1998
220 killed and 5,000 wounded

# MURDERER
## *Usama Bin Laden*
### UP TO $5 MILLION REWARD

Usama Bin Laden and Muhammad Atef have been indicted for the August 7, 1998 bombings of the U.S. embassies in Kenya and Tanzania. These brutal attacks killed more than 220 innocent Americans, Kenyans and Tanzanians and seriously injured more than 5,000 men, women and children.

Bin Laden, Atef, and their organization, al Qaeda, also allegedly conspired in the killings of American military personnel in Saudi Arabia and Somalia.

To preserve the peace and save innocent lives from further attacks, the U.S. Government is offering a reward for information leading to the arrest or conviction of Bin Laden and Atef. Persons providing information may be eligible for a reward of up to $5 million, protection of their identities, and may be eligible for relocation of themselves and their families. Persons wishing to report information on Usama Bin Laden, Muhammad Atef, or other terrorists, should contact the authorities or the nearest U.S. embassy or consulate.

Within the United States, contact the Federal Bureau of Investigation or call the U.S. Department of State, Diplomatic Security Service at 1-800-HEROES-1. Information may also be provided by contacting:

### HEROES
Post Office Box 96781
Washington, D.C. 20090-6781 U.S.A.
email:heroes@heroes.net
www.heroes.net

# UP TO $5 MILLION REWARD
# ABSOLUTE CONFIDENTIALITY

sometimes called on them to assist in operations elsewhere.

Overthrowing the house of al-Saud and establishing a genuine Islamic fundamentalist government there was a goal that was especially meaningful for bin Laden. Yet as the Islamic fundamentalist leadership mapped out its priorities, Egypt became the prime target. There was a good reason for this. If Saudi Arabia's rulers had to deal with an Islamic uprising, it was likely that Egypt would come to their aid. However, if Egypt were thrust into a state of internal chaos first, it probably would not have any resources to spare.

Osama bin Laden was among those who helped determine the course of the Islamic revolution's invigorated Middle East campaign. They decided on a highly visible target, reasoning that the greater the disruption caused, the more it would work to their advantage. Therefore, the terrorists decided to assassinate Egyptian President Hosni Mubarak when he visited Ethiopia in June 1997.

In many ways Mubarak was a perfect mark for bin Laden and his cohorts since Islamic fundamentalists felt that the Egyptian leader's policies mirrored all that was wrong with secular governments in the Middle

*A poster issued by the U.S. State Department in January 1999*

East. Islamic fundamentalists had assassinated his predecessor, Anwar Sadat, in 1981 after Sadat had taken steps toward a lasting peace with Israel. To their disappointment, when Mubarak took office he seemed to pick up where Sadat left off. The new Egyptian president used the Egyptian police and the nation's intelligence service to repress Islamic fundamentalists there as well. He also pledged to help any government in the region threatened by an Islamic revolutionary upheaval.

Mubarak honored the peace his predecessor forged with Israel and worked to cement a close relationship with the United States as well. Under Mubarak, Egypt was also a leading nation in ushering the United States into the region during the Gulf War. To Islamic fundamentalists, Hosni Mubarak was not a Muslim leader but a Western-dominated puppet. They hoped that his elimination would send a signal to others that there was no longer any room for someone like him in the Muslim world.

The assassination mission involved a substantial group of Islamic revolutionaries from a number of different countries. This was done to make it difficult for Egyptian and Western intelligence agents to trace the plot's origins. Nevertheless, it would later be disclosed that many of those participating in the plot had been trained at camps operated by bin Laden's group, al-Qaeda.

Despite months of planning, the attempt failed and Mubarak escaped unharmed. Yet the Islamic revolutionaries felt that Egypt was still not lost to them. They believed that there was a growing trend in the country toward fundamentalist thinking and that the assassination attempt had boosted the hopes of those supporting it. Islamic revolutionaries would exploit that sentiment in the months ahead, often carrying out small attacks on tourists. Targeting tourists accomplished a dual purpose. They could make it unpleasant or even frightening for Westerners to vacation in Egypt as well as hurt its economy in doing so.

Bin Laden and others close to him hoped that Egypt would now be too occupied with its own problems to come to Saudi Arabia's aid once they struck there. In fact, they were counting on it when they planned to bomb a U.S. military training center in Riyadh, Saudi Arabia, where American personnel trained the Saudi National Guard. Considered an ideal choice because it would hurt the United States as well as the house of al-Saud, bin Laden had both selected the target and mapped out the detailed plan.

At this juncture in his career, bin Laden also took on a somewhat new role in that he began drafting a number of the critical communiqués that would be publicly aired after the bombing. Some authorities claim that in time they were able to recognize bin Laden's distinctive writing style and could detect his "voice" in future briefings of this nature.

While Islamic militants like bin Laden saw the West as a threat to Islam, they nevertheless made full use of

Western technology in furthering their agenda. Osama bin Laden was well versed in computers and relied heavily on the Internet for recruitment as well as for administrative communications. Much later it would be learned that the Federal Bureau of Investigations (FBI) thwarted several of his terrorist plots by wire tapping bin Laden's e-mail.

Although the terrorists had failed with their prime Egyptian target, they were far more successful in Saudi Arabia. On November 3, 1995, a large group of Americans were enjoying lunch at the military training base when a car bomb blew up in the parking lot. Within seconds a portion of the building and close to fifty cars had turned to rubble. A few minutes later a second blast went off, killing and wounding still more people. In the end, seven people died and over sixty were injured.

Bin Laden's expertise in the endeavor was obvious. Investigators described the strike as methodically planned and executed. A knowledgeable Saudi source in London noted that "those who carried out the explosion have a very advanced security and political sense. They chose a U.S. target in the heart of Riyadh City in order to attract the biggest amount possible of world media attention and to cause a huge political furor." The source added that the explosives had served as a "clear message to the Americans to the effect that the regime [the House of al-Saud] is not in control and [is] unstable."[1]

Another source added that the Riyadh operation had been "designed to draw attention to the fact that the arrival in Saudi Arabia of the technology of booby-trapped cars [sophisticated bomb-making techniques] is a serious turning point which could have repercussions." The source further stressed that "oil installations could become potential targets in the future to ensure the largest possible amount of world publicity."[2]

Confessions of four men later arrested for the bombing were aired on Saudi television. They admitted having been influenced by faxes sent from a fundamentalist group bin Laden was associated with. By then, U.S. intelligence experts strongly suspected that Osama bin Laden's involvement was more significant, and one official noted that "bin Laden was 'high up on our suspect list' of those responsible for the bombing."[3]

Though bin Laden was safely back at his home in Sudan at the time of the bombing, he would not escape the wrath of the house of al-Saud. High-ranking Saudi officials hoped to curtail bin Laden's terrorist plans for Saudi Arabia by delivering a meaningful "warning."[4] On a morning shortly after the Riyadh bombing, a 1981 Toyota pickup truck stopped in front of Osama bin Laden's residence. Four mercenaries from Yemen with AK-47 assault rifles then opened fire on the house and several of bin Laden's bodyguards stationed outside it. The bodyguards returned fire, and by the time it was over, three of the assailants and two of the body-guards were dead. The surviving mercenary was arrested and quickly executed by the Sudanese government.

From that day on Osama bin Laden's house and street were transformed into an armed camp of sorts. A ring of barriers was immediately erected to protect his dwelling, and armed guards were stationed both around the house and along the street on a twenty-four-hour basis. To make it impossible for unauthorized vehicles to enter the vicinity, expansive trenches were also dug at both ends of the street. Not even pedestrians walking along the road were spared the scrutiny of bin Laden's protective team. Such individuals would be stopped, questioned, and searched before being permitted to continue on their way. All these precautions were provided by the Sudanese government, which spared no expense in guarding its terrorist treasure.

Osama bin Laden would need all the protection he could get. Even prior to the Riyadh bombing, the CIA had connected him to "numerous terrorist organizations" and believed he was responsible for providing "funding and other logistic support through his companies to a number of extremist causes."[5] But in the early 1990s, bin Laden's participation was believed to be largely financial. One CIA official is quoted as saying, "The conventional wisdom at the time was that he was some sort of financier and little else, a kind of

Gucci [fashionable] terrorist. [But] the more we dug, the more it became clear that there was more."[6]

Although for years Osama bin Laden had successfully used his international affiliations and business connections to camouflage his terrorist involvement, his cover was unraveling. The CIA had now begun to realize that it might be dealing with an individual whose intelligence and public image were as important to the Islamic fundamentalist revolution as his money. In January 1996 the agency formed a special Osama bin Laden task force, believing that he posed a serious international threat.

Since bin Laden had gone to great lengths to cover his tracks, it was not going to be easy for the CIA to learn about him. The task ahead proved to be time consuming and expensive. In fact, it was the most costly investigation ever launched into a single person suspected of terrorist activities. While the stereotype of intelligence work involves the cloak-and-dagger intrigue of infiltrating clandestine groups and working with informants, in reality, there is usually also a good deal of tedious paperwork to plow through. This was especially true in investigating Osama bin Laden, since much of his financial and political dealings had been purposely disguised to thwart detection. "The initial work on bin Laden was really boring," one source with the CIA noted. "The guys [in the counterterrorism center] read and digested everything bin Laden had ever said or written."[7]

Their hard work paid off. It wasn't long before some very damaging revelations about bin Laden's life and business dealings came to light. Among other things, intelligence agents found that there was still a number of high-ranking Saudi politicians and successful businessmen who had remained quietly loyal to Osama bin Laden and continued to funnel a flow of cash to him in Sudan. There were also substantial sums secretly coming bin Laden's way from affluent and influential individuals in Kuwait and Qatar. These were nations that had depended on U.S. might in the Gulf War and continued to do so afterward. Now the embarrassing news of the bin Laden backers put these countries under tremendous pressure to help bring the wanted terrorist to justice.

That set the stage for a U.S. Special Forces operation to be launched. Its aim was to use the military to capture bin Laden while he was secretly visiting his backers in the Persian Gulf area. The countries in question had agreed to cooperate. Having been exposed as assisting him, nations still dependent on the United States were not about to offer bin Laden a safe harbor at their expense. Only one thing stood in the way of the mission's success. Through his own intelligence sources, bin Laden learned what was happening and refused to venture out of Sudan.

Since Sudan was an Islamic state with bin Laden's mentor and friend Hassan al-Turabi at its spiritual helm, it looked as though the United States would have to wait for its prey. Help from an Islamic state where bin Laden was well received seemed highly unlikely. Kenneth Katzman, terrorism expert for the Congressional Research Service, described the bin Laden/Turabi relationship this way: "Bin Laden is inspired by Turabi's expansive vision; he sees eye to eye with him. Turabi has Islamic credentials bin Laden could never have. They are allies. They are close associates. They are business partners. Bin Laden is Turabi's alter ego, his field commander, his operations chief."[8]

Yet Osama bin Laden was not quite as safe as some might suppose. In 1996 there was a second assassination attempt on his life. While there is not a great deal of information available on the incident, it is rumored that one of his bodyguards turned on bin Laden at the behest of the Saudi regime. When that didn't work, Saudi officials went to Sudan to deliver an ultimatum to Hassan al-Turabi. Speaking for America, they warned the cleric that unless he gave up bin Laden, Sudan would have to face U.S. economic sanctions. At first, Turabi remained loyal to both his cause and bin Laden, who'd been a valued protégé. Nevertheless, he soon realized that the consequences of sheltering Osama bin Laden did not justify the gains. In the spring of 1996 he regretfully asked bin Laden to find another sanctuary.

Having been politely ousted from Sudan while pursued by the CIA, Osama bin Laden's residential choices had become extremely narrowed. In contemplating what was available to him, the newspaper *Al Quds al-Arabi* quoted bin Laden as saying, "Iraq is out of the question. I would rather die than live in a European state [a country steeped in Western ways]. I have to live in a Muslim country and so the choice is between Yemen and Afghanistan."[9]

His ultimate choice was Afghanistan, a now strict Islamic fundamentalist country ruled by the Taliban. Afghanistan was an ideal place for Osama bin Laden at this point in his life. During the 1980s he had fought there to oust the Soviets and establish its Islamic regime. Osama bin Laden was still highly respected in Afghanistan and had many close friends and ties throughout the country.

Support for Osama bin Laden in Afghanistan was so great, as a matter of fact, that it would be nearly impossible for U.S. forces to penetrate his defenses there. When the United States pressured Sudan to expel the dangerous terrorist, officials had not realized that bin Laden would find a new, even more secure arena from which to operate. As it turned out, it didn't take bin Laden long to resume a number of ongoing operations from his new home. He arrived in Afghanistan with his wives and children in May 1996, and the following month he is believed to have supported members of the al Qaeda organization and others in a bombing that took the lives of nineteen people and injured many more.

The attack occurred on June 25 in Dhahran, Saudi Arabia. A huge truck bomb exploded near a U.S. military housing unit known as Khobar Towers. The extent of Osama bin Laden's participation has never been fully determined, but once again U.S. officials immediately suspected his involvement and there's evidence indicating that they were right. Telephone calls intercepted by the authorities revealed that close associates of bin Laden called to congratulate him on the attack just days later. Yet other sources claim that bin Laden offered only his advice in this incident.

Bin Laden denied having anything to do with the bombing, though as usual few in U.S. intelligence believed him. Nevertheless, bin Laden made a point of publicly praising the terrorists who successfully carried out the mission. "Only Americans were killed in the explosions," he commented. "No Saudi citizen suffered any injury. When I got the news about these blasts, I was very happy. This was a noble act. This was a great honor but, unfortunately, I did not conduct these explosions personally. But I would like to say to the Saudi people that they should adopt every tactic to throw the Americans out of Saudi territory."[10]

Osama bin Laden and other Islamic revolutionaries were not hesitant about openly offering the world an explanation for the escalation of violence in the Middle East. Abdul-Bari Atwan, a good friend of bin Laden's as well as editor of *Al Quds al-Arabi*, expressed it in an editorial, which squarely placed the blame on the

United States. It read: "If those who killed the Americans in Saudi Arabia and Cairo [the attacks on Western tourists] belong to the Islamic extremist camp, it was Washington, its policies and its allies in the region that created this phenomenon and supplied it with fuel needed for its expansion in the region as a whole."[11]

Now safely ensconced in Afghanistan, Osama bin Laden finally began to realize his full potential as an international leader of the Islamic extremist movement. Yet to stay alive while fulfilling this role, it was necessary for him to remain surrounded by a substantial number of bodyguards. He established a three-room operations base in a cave that had been carved out of a mountainside. It was a modest site with few creature comforts. The furniture consisted of a few crude beds built low to the ground with thinly worn mattresses and two shelves of Islamic texts. The only touches present of the high-tech world that bin Laden depended on to help orchestrate an international jihad were his satellite phone and two laptop computers. These surroundings lack any hint of the luxury that Osama bin Laden was accustomed to.

"It was freezing," one editor at *Al Quds al-Arabi* said in describing the rustic surroundings after he'd visited bin Laden for an interview. "I reached under my camp bed hoping to find an extra blanket. Instead it was crammed with Kalashnikov rifles and mortar bombs."[12]

Nevertheless, establishing an operations base in a cave offered excellent camouflage as well as protection from possible U.S. air attacks. Bin Laden kept a small army of soldiers to protect his mountain base around the clock. Anyone who wanted to penetrate bin Laden's newest headquarters would have to get past hundreds of fighters armed with AK-47s as well as an array of tanks.

While those were his unofficial headquarters, that was not the only cave in Afghanistan where Osama bin Laden worked or lived in. Sources close to him indicated that for security reasons he rarely remained in any one location for more than two or three days at a time. Moving about the countryside, no one person ever knew the precise placement of all his hideouts or where he would be on a given day. Yet bin Laden never traveled to any of these places alone. He rode from location to location in an armed convoy equipped with an array of weapons, which included rocket launchers and Stinger surface to air missiles.

Osama bin Laden thought the probability of a U.S. air attack against him was high and with good cause. In July 1996, during an interview with British journalist Robert Fisk, bin Laden made his anti-American feelings frighteningly clear. He said that in his estimation the Riyadh and Khobar Towers bombings were actually "the beginning of a war between Muslims and the United States."[13] When further questioned as to whether he was declaring war on the West, bin Laden responded, "It is not a declaration of war—it's a real description of the situation. It doesn't mean declaring war against the West and Western people—but against

the American regime which is against every Muslim. . . .
The explosion in Khobar did not come as a direct reac-
tion to American occupation but as a result of American
behavior against Muslims, its support of Jews in
Palestine and of the massacres [by Jews] of Muslims in
Palestine and Lebanon. . . ."[14]

Bin Laden used the same interview to warn other
Western nations not to follow in the U.S.'s footsteps:
"Now let me give some advice to the governments of
Britain and France to take their troops out—because
what happened in Riyadh and Khobar showed that the
people who did this have a deep understanding in
choosing their targets. They hit their main enemy,
which is Americans. They killed no secondary enemies,
nor their brothers in the army or the police of Saudi
Arabia. I give this advice to the government of
Britain."[15]

When Osama bin Laden warned Britain to stay out
of the Persian Gulf area, he and his associates were
already working on forming a broad anti-Western
international coalition. In February 1998, bin Laden
concluded strategy meetings with a number of other
prominent Islamic fundamentalist leaders and
announced that the coalition was to be known as the
International Islamic Front for Jihad Against Jews and
Crusaders. The group's stated purpose, which was
largely written by bin Laden, was as follows:

> For over seven years the United States has
> been occupying the lands of Islam in the

holiest of places, the Arabian Peninsula, plundering its riches, dictating to its rulers, humiliating its people, terrorizing its neighbors, and turning its bases in the peninsula into a spearhead through which to fight the neighboring Muslim peoples. Good Muslims must fight and kill American civilians and soldiers wherever they can in accordance with the words of Almighty God.[16]

If there was ever even the slightest doubt left about Osama bin Laden's involvement in terrorist activities or what his intentions toward the United States were, it no longer existed. In essence, bin Laden was urging his supporters to murder Americans wherever they found them. As might be expected, the document caused quite a stir in Washington, D.C. Intelligence agents knew that they were not facing an idle threat. Osama bin Laden was a well organized and highly intelligent foe, and the CIA suspected that it would not be long before they'd be dealing with this terrorist's actions instead of his words. As a result, government officials intensified efforts to apprehend the millionaire outlaw, who by now ranked among the most popular Islamic revolutionary leaders in the world.

They began by having diplomats venture into Afghanistan in March 1998 to talk secretly with high-ranking Taliban members. They were there to let it be known that America would pay a sizable sum to anyone willing to betray Osama bin Laden by turning him over to them. There was also another reason for Taliban members to do so. The Taliban had long wanted its regime to be recognized by the UN as Afghanistan's legitimate government. This would be impossible as long as it continued to harbor an internationally-sought terrorist. Neither of these incentives worked, however. Osama bin Laden remained protected by his followers and the diplomats left empty-handed.

There were other attempts to bring bin Laden in as well. In April 1998, Bill Richardson, former U.S. ambassador to the UN, flew to Afghanistan to try to make still another deal with the Taliban. At the same time, U.S. Special Forces had been dispatched to the area to see if they could pull off a "snatch" operation to bring the infamous bin Laden to justice. But both of these attempts were unsuccessful.

Osama bin Laden was not oblivious to the pressure put on the Taliban to give him up. In the spring of 1998 he supposedly called on Taliban head Mullah Mohammed Omar and offered to leave the country if his presence in Afghanistan was making it too difficult for the regime. Bin Laden's offer was declined as the Mullah reassuringly told him, "You are one of our own and you will remain."[17]

# The Fight
# Intensifies

OSAMA BIN LADEN KNEW THAT TO validate his February 1998 international call to kill Americans, he would need to set an example. U.S. government officials expected a strike, they just weren't sure where or when it would occur. As it turned out, they would not have to wait long for a horrific event. Bin Laden had already zeroed in on American targets in Kenya and Tanzania.

In many parts of the world, bin Laden would leave small units of his terrorist organization al Qaeda ready to spring into action. While waiting, members of this terrorist group lived quiet, seemingly normal lives. They ran businesses, had families, and to an outsider seemed fairly average. Yet they were actually loyal Islamic revolutionaries and when needed to assist in a

assist in a terrorist mission, they were prepared to do whatever was asked of them. In 2001 he would call on such individuals to strike in New York City and Washington, D.C. But in 1998 bin Laden activated his followers in Africa.

Bin Laden's plan was to bomb two U.S. embassies in different African countries. The explosions were to occur on August 7, 1998, within ten minutes of one another. He put together an elaborate scheme to achieve this, and it paid off. Preparations had begun nearly a year beforehand by having the terrorist cell rent a villa in Nairobi, Kenya. The two-story dwelling was surrounded by a tall wall and hedge. It was an ideal setting for them since what went on inside remained well hidden from view. At the villa, the men involved worked on the details of the plan and made sure that each one knew precisely what he was to do.

One of the men Osama bin Laden relied on here was Mohammed Sadiq Odeh, a young Islamic extremist who had trained in Afghanistan and was fiercely loyal to bin Laden. Odeh had been instructed to see that the details of the operation were in proper order and that nothing had been left to chance. On the eve of the bombing, once he was certain that the group was ready, bin Laden had Odeh leave the area.

*Medical personnel carry a victim to a waiting ambulance amid the wreckage at the American Embassy in Nairobi, Kenya, after it was bombed on August 7, 1998.*

Traveling under a different name with a fraudulent passport, Odeh fled to Pakistan as instructed.

Another key person in the plot was Fazul Abdullah Mohammed, who had been active in al Qaeda for some time. Most recently he'd been sent to Kenya to establish himself there and wait for further directions. Two other people pivotal to the plot were a man known as Azzam, and Mohamed Rashed Daoud Al-'Owhali, who had personally begged bin Laden to be allowed to participate in a mission. The night before the strike, the pair had made a video to celebrate their forthcoming martyrdom in the suicide mission bin Laden had planned.

There were to be two trucks involved in the bombing attack. The first vehicle would simply drive past the embassy. It was to be a decoy of sorts. The second would be carrying a bomb containing two thousand pounds of TNT—this truck would stop in front of the embassy.

At 10:30 A.M. the truck carrying the bomb reached its destination. Azzam was driving, while Al-'Owhali was a passenger. Al-'Owhali jumped from the vehicle and threw a grenade to distract the Kenyan security guard posted outside the embassy. Seconds later, Azzam opened fire at the embassy's window. Meanwhile, Al-'Owhali had already started running down the street when Azzam set off the bomb. Though Al-'Owhali received a deep wound in his back, he would later confess to authorities that he ran away at the last minute because he had changed his mind about becoming a martyr.

Others at the site didn't have that option. The blast destroyed the embassy, killing over 213 innocent people and injuring at least 4,500 more. As planned, Azzam, the suicide bomber, died as well. Moments later, another blast went off 415 miles away at the U.S. Embassy in Dar es Salaam, Tanzania. This time 11 people were killed and 85 injured.

Oneko Aura, a reporter for Nairobi Television, was doing an interview only blocks from the embassy when the bomb went off in Kenya. He recalled the hideous event as follows: "It was reminiscent of doomsday. The first thing I saw was a thick cloud of smoke billowing above my head. Minutes later, I saw people running, bleeding profusely."[1]

Not surprisingly, authorities investigating the bombings suspected that bin Laden was behind them. "He was at the top of our short list," a source close to the investigations remarked.[2] It wasn't long before their suspicions were confirmed. Mohammed Sadiq Odeh was questioned at the airport in Pakistan when his flight from Nairobi landed there. He had been picked up after immigration officials realized that he was traveling with a false passport. During interrogation, Odeh admitted to being an explosives expert and acknowledged that he had acquired his skills at one of bin Laden's training bases. Before long he confessed to his role in the Nairobi bombing adding, "I did it all for the cause of Islam. [Osama bin Laden] is my leader and I obey his orders."[3] Mohammed Sadiq Odeh would later be deported to the United States to stand trial.

Al-'Owhali was also picked up by authorities shortly after the bombing. Doctors at the hospital where he was treated for his back wound had suspected that something was wrong. The type of injury he sustained had to occur while he was running away from the blast—not as a result of being in the middle of things. Feeling certain that he was involved in the bombing, the hospital staff alerted police. During questioning, Al-'Owhali confessed, revealing a good deal of valuable information about the plot. In discussing his conclusions about the bombing, Detective Peter Mbuvi of Kenya's National Police said, "Investigators have revealed so far . . . that most of the people who are behind this incident, actually, they have all been financed by Osama bin Laden."[4]

True to character, Osama bin Laden denied masterminding the bombings. "I heard about the bombings the same way everyone else heard about them, from television or radio," he told a reporter months after the incident. "I did not order them but was very glad for what happened to the Americans there. [The bombings] were Islamic revenge on the American spies in East Africa. Many oppressed Muslims are ready to die in the war against the Americans. Those who did it may be some of these oppressed Muslims."[5]

Even after bin Laden was told that Mohammed Sadiq Odeh had implicated him in the bombings, the terrorist leader persisted in his denial. "[Odeh] was tortured in Pakistan and Kenya and therefore his so-called confession is meaningless," he replied. "It indicates the failure of American intelligence in the world. The American president and his administration are under the influence of the Jewish Zionist lobby in America who are pushing the American people to do what Israel cannot do."[6]

Osama bin Laden's denials did not carry very much weight with the U.S. government. On August 20, 1998, it retaliated with an air strike known as Operation Infinite Reach. Five U.S. warships were strategically placed in both the Arabian and the Red seas. During the military maneuvers, over eighty Tomahawk missiles were fired at a number of strategic targets in Afghanistan and Sudan.

These included three terrorist training bases in Afghanistan. The bases were used by a number of groups associated with bin Laden. It was no secret that the attack's primary objective had been to directly hit Osama bin Laden himself.

That day the terrorist leader had been scheduled to visit and dine with several of his key commanders at one of the targeted training camps. Had he not unexpectedly postponed this item on his Thursday agenda at the last minute, it is likely that the men would have been sipping after-dinner *kahwa* (Arabic coffee) when the bombs fell. Realizing that it was in pursuit of an extremely elusive target who is well insulated and protected by the Taliban, the United States stepped up its efforts in its war against Osama bin Laden.

In November 1998, Osama bin Laden was charged by a federal grand jury with directing a worldwide terrorist ring that carried out the bombings of the embassies in Kenya and Tanzania. He was also charged with promoting attacks on U.S. troops in Somalia and Saudi Arabia since 1991. To encourage his apprehension, the U.S. State Department offered rewards of up to $5 million for information leading to his capture.

Mohammed Sadiq Odeh, Mohamed Rashid Daoud Al-'Owhali, and others who had been charged earlier in connection with the African embassy bombings were now indicted along with bin Laden. "Our investigating strategy is clear," noted Lewis D. Shiliro, assistant director of the FBI office directing the Osama bin Laden investigation. "We will identify, locate and prosecute all those responsible right down the line, from those who constructed and developed bombs to those who paid for them and ordered it done."[7] The FBI was true to its word. In February 2001, bin Laden's indicted accomplices went on trial for the bombings. They were convicted.

Further direct action was taken in an attempt to hamstring Osama bin Laden financially as well. On August 28, 1998, the same day the United States launched Operation Infinite Reach, President Bill Clinton amended Executive Order 12947, a 1995 order barring business with Middle Eastern terrorist groups, to include Osama bin Laden and key individuals in his al Qaeda group. According to the State Department, this blocked "their U.S. assets—including property and bank accounts." It also prohibited any "transactions or dealings with them by United States persons or within the United States."[8]

The president further explained the effort in his weekly radio address noting, "We must not allow sanctuary for terrorism; not for terrorists or their money. It takes money, lots of it, to build the network bin Laden has. We'll do our best to see that he has less of it."[9]

A senior administration official added, "The effect of this action is to expose the network, the organization, in a very public way. The object is to take down the infrastructure."[10]

Yet the ban was not expected to result in any immediate, dramatic consequences. It was fairly well known that Osama bin Laden did not keep a significant portion of his wealth in the United States. Intelligence sources had learned that he had even moved much of his funding out of Britain and had confined the bulk of his banking to Asian nations.

Bin Laden had also extensively diversified his investments, making it especially difficult to track the companies holding his assets or know where he was regarded as a principal financial backer. "He's got a wide array of diverse companies in which he's invested in to some degree or controls outright," explained one U.S. official. "They run the gamut from agricultural companies to banking and investment firms to construction companies, and they hide many kinds of export-import companies."[11]

Meanwhile, the U.S. government tried other ways to stop Osama bin Laden. Acting on information supplied by spies who had successfully infiltrated bin Laden's terrorist organization, twenty of the terrorist's key people in twenty-eight countries were arrested and questioned. The United States was also thought to have supported Prince Salaman bin Abdul-Aziz of Saudi Arabia, the governor of Riyadh, in a 1998 covert attempt on Osama bin Laden's life. The prince supposedly paid an assassin over a quarter of a million dollars to poison bin Laden. The scheme only partially worked. Bin Laden went into acute kidney failure, but survived.

For months afterward, a weakened and seemingly frail bin Laden used a cane to get around. There were rumors that he was dying of kidney disease. His weakened condition further sparked the rumor that he was suffering from cancer, but this was never confirmed. Increasingly mindful of plots against him, bin Laden further enhanced his already tight security. When a group of assassins approached his cave in December 1998, they were speedily disposed of. In the event that

Osama bin Laden was ever about to be captured by U.S. or other enemy agents, his men were to ensure that he would not be taken alive. His bodyguards were ordered to shoot him if escape was impossible. (His oldest son is among the men who guard him.) Bin Laden was actually doubly protected—with both his own bodyguards and the Taliban looking after him.

However, in March 1999, Osama bin Laden and his Taliban protectors supposedly had a violent falling out. It was reported that a fight broke out between bin Laden's hand-picked personal bodyguards and the Taliban officers assigned to protect him. As a result, bin Laden was expelled from the region of Afghanistan where he had been staying with his family and sent to hide out in a more isolated and desolate portion of the country. It was also said that the terrorist's cell phone had been confiscated.

American officials were encouraged by this action, as they had argued for some time that Osama bin Laden regularly used the phone to plan international terrorist acts. "There is friction between him and the Taliban," a senior American officer said in describing the situation. "They have tried to constrain him for the first time and tried to limit his communications. It's a good sign."[12]

Soon afterward, there was talk of Osama bin Laden voluntarily leaving Afghanistan to seek asylum in Iraq under the protection of Saddam Hussein. Though bin Laden and Hussein had formerly been at odds, their relationship had mellowed over time. Other sources, however, claimed that bin Laden's communications with Hussein may have had more to do with possibly obtaining chemical and biological weapons than with finding a new sanctuary.

Despite any disputes he may have had with them, Osama bin Laden described his and his followers' relationship with the Taliban in a positive light: "We support the Taliban and we consider ourselves part of them," he noted. "Our blood is mixed with the blood of our Afghan brothers. For us, there is only one government in Afghanistan. It is the Taliban government. We obey all its orders. Afghanistan was the place where we buried the Soviet Union and it will be the place to bury the Americans for their designs on Muslims."[13]

Since the Taliban in Afghanistan refused to give bin Laden up, the United States also imposed sanctions against that regime. In July 1999, through an executive order, all Taliban assets in the United States were frozen and all trade with Afghanistan was banned until the regime agreed to surrender Osama bin Laden to a nation where he can face justice. This move has been somewhat effective. According to the State Department, by August 2000 "$250 million in assets [had] been frozen and fund transfers in which the Taliban have an interest amounting to $1.6 million in assets have been frozen. These measures . . . are causing governments and companies to avoid doing business with the Taliban."[14]

The effect of the U.S. sanctions was enhanced in October 1999 when the UN Security Council passed a resolution imposing international sanctions on Afghanistan until the Taliban turns over Osama bin Laden. The sanctions, which took effect the following month, curtailed international flights by Ariana, Afghanistan's national airline, as well as froze Taliban assets in many parts of the world.

Nevertheless, the imposed sanctions have failed to break the Taliban's resolve. "We are sticking to our principles," Wakil Ahmed Mutawakkel, a Taliban minister, told a newspaper reporter in the Arab Emirates. "We refuse to hand over bin Laden to an infidel state."[15] Taliban leader Mullah Mohammed Omar reiterated these sentiments when he publicly stated that the United States "will wait in vain" for the regime to turn in "one of its greatest."[16] It was also rumored that the bond between the Taliban leader and bin Laden was further strengthened when the Mullah recently married bin Laden's oldest daughter.

Indeed, loyalty to bin Laden and rancor against the West remained strong among both Taliban soldiers and Afghanistan residents. For two days following the imposed UN sanctions, there were protests in the streets. Demonstrators shouted "Down with America" and threw stones at the local UN office. Still others burned an American flag. "We will not be bullied by an imperialist UN and United States," Zia Naeemir, a forty-two-year-old protestor shouted. "We will take out our wrath on America and its supporters."

Naeemir was among the men who had offered to "carry a bomb into the streets of America" for Osama bin Laden."[17]

Osama bin Laden also remains very much a hero to Islamic youths. This is especially true of those who attend the Muslim religious seminaries run by Islamic fundamentalists. These schools, called *madrassans*, cull their students from the poorest echelons of society. Their room, board, and tuition are free. The male student body, which ranges in age from about nine to thirty, is taught that the answers to all of society's problems lie in Islamic fundamentalism. These learning institutions have frequently been characterized as early training grounds for holy fighters. Indeed, many of the young men later go on to one of the terrorist training bases established by Osama bin Laden.

Along with studying the Koran, students at these schools learn that bin Laden is a leader of heroic stature to be emulated. As Wali, one such student at a school in Pakistan, told a visiting reporter, "Osama bin Laden is a great Muslim. The West is afraid of Muslims, so they made him their enemy. Osama wants to keep Islam pure from the pollution of the infidels. He [Osama bin Laden] believes Islam is the way for all the world."[18]

There, as in many similar institutions, the school's pride and even the students' sense of worth and identity appear innately bound up with Osama bin

Laden—a man seen as someone who can do no wrong. When the reporter asked the youths at the same school if they hoped to see Osama bin Laden armed with nuclear weapons, every hand in the room went up and some students even applauded. The reporter further questioned the students as to what they would do if Osama bin Laden was captured and brought to America to stand trial. A student named Mohammed, who answered for the class, said, "We would sacrifice our lives for Osama. We would kill Americans."[19] Asked what kind of Americans— meaning soldiers or civilians—Mohammed simply replied, "All Americans."

Osama bin Laden may have done even more damage than is generally realized. The seed of future jihads may already be sown.

# 10
# The Challenge Ahead

FOLLOWING THE 1998 U.S. EMBASSY bombings in Africa, Osama bin Laden remained the emir general, or head, of an international terrorist network that continued to actively plot against the West. While never losing control of the overall planning objectives, bin Laden frequently delegated a good deal of the responsibility to high-powered commanders around the globe. Among the top men in his organization was Mohammed Atef, a former Egyptian policeman, who was instrumental in developing the military aspects of the organization. The men became in-laws in January 2001, when bin Laden's son married Atef's daughter.

*Even if Osama bin Laden is captured and brought to justice, it is likely that there is a vast supply of equally zealous jihadists to step in and take his place. This bin Laden supporter was photographed at an anti-U.S. rally in Pakistan in 1999.*

**125**

In many ways Osama bin Laden's terrorist associates had replaced his extended family in Saudi Arabia. The bin Ladens, who still had business dealings with both Saudi Arabia's rulers and the West, had disowned Osama years earlier.

Dr. Ayman al Zawahiri was like another surrogate relative to Osama bin Laden. Through the years, al Zawahiri continued to be one of bin Laden's most trusted advisers. Al Zawahiri founded the Egyptian terrorist group Islamic Jihad, which to some degree had effectively merged with al Qaeda. If bin Laden was regarded by the West as Public Enemy Number One, then al Zawahiri was Public Enemy Number Two. Some speculated that if anything happened to bin Laden, al Zawahiri would step into his shoes. However, those shoes would be hard to fill.

Osama bin Laden's status as a legend continued to grow. Throughout much of the Middle East a cultlike admiration surrounded bin Laden as he became the ultimate symbol of courage and daring in standing up to the West. Vendors in the Gulf region were often unable to meet the demand for stickers and posters bearing his image as well as books and tapes containing his speeches. Numerous Islamic fundamentalist couples began naming their babies Osama. Bin Laden's following was well aware of his exploits and applauded his achievements.

Osama bin Laden was connected to the October 12, 2000, bombing attack on the U.S. Navy destroyer the U.S.S. *Cole*. The ship had stopped to refuel in the port of Aden, Yemen, when terrorists blasted it, killing seventeen sailors. An unsettling videotape had turned up just before the *Cole* tragedy. In it bin Laden called for additional action in Yemen. He also wore a traditional Yemeni dagger, which he had never been photographed with previously. It proved to be an ominous warning of things to come. A similar video-tape surfaced in the summer of 2001 in which bin Laden encouraged followers to destroy the United States and Israel. Aimed at young Muslim males, in some ways it served as a powerful recruitment tool for bin Laden's organization. Shortly after its release, the September 11, 2001, attacks on the United States took place.

Bin Laden has also been tied to other terrorist plots that fortunately were foiled by law enforcement agencies. These included schemes to bomb still other U.S. embassies as well as the Prince Sultan Air Base in Saudi Arabia. Bin Laden had planned an explosion in Seattle during the New Year's Eve celebration for the year 2000, along with a number of other millennium attacks that night. He was behind a plan to blow up Australia's only nuclear reactor during the Summer 2000 Olympic Games as well. That plot was uncovered accidentally while New Zealand police were looking into an illegal immigration ring involving Afghan refugees.

Unfortunately, the execution of the September 11 assaults wasn't stopped. The horrific events served as a wake-up call for all Americans. They wondered what else the terrorist leader might have in store for them. It was a well-known fact that for some time Osama bin Laden had been actively trying to acquire instruments of mass destruction (chemical, nuclear, and biological weapons) for use against U.S. interests. Bin Laden had previously expressed his reasoning behind resorting to unconventional weaponry, publicly stating, "Acquiring [chemical, nuclear, and biological weapons] for the defense of Muslims is a religious duty. If I have indeed acquired these weapons then I thank God for enabling me to do so." [1]

Intelligence sources discovered that bin Laden had attempted to buy deadly biological weapons such as anthrax and plague viruses from dealers in the former Soviet Union. It was also believed that he had developed ties with Sudanese individuals involved in the production of chemical weapons. Satellite images from terrorist training camps in Afghanistan even yielded pictures of dead animals on test ranges, indicating that the terrorists had experimented with poisonous gas.

In the United States, a crop duster plane manual was found after the September 11 attacks in one of the terrorists' hideouts and it was learned that terrorists had inquired about the operation of these small planes at a Florida crop dusting company. In the wrong hands, such aircraft could be used to dispense biological or chemical agents. Authorities believe that bin Laden's group also wanted to use weapons of mass destruction on the ground. Several suspected terrorists in the United States illegally obtained licenses to haul hazardous materials. Bin Laden operatives were also thought to have been involved with the cases of the potentially deadly disease anthrax that began to surface a month after the attacks.

Yet if bin Laden and his organization had become stronger and more strategic, so had U.S. efforts to stop him. President George W. Bush promised that the September 11, 2001, attack on the United States would not go unpunished. Putting the Taliban on notice, the president further stressed that the United States would not distinguish between those guilty of the actual deeds and those who harbored them. The United States had been attacked and was now at war. This war would be different from any it had ever waged. The war against Osama bin Laden and his international terrorist network would not be fought strictly with guns, tanks, and missiles. There would be political and economic aspects as well.

This war was to be waged both at home and abroad. A $25 million reward was offered for bin Laden and his cohorts. U.S. Attorney General John Ashcroft also initiated the largest investigation in the history of the United States to identify members of bin Laden's network. Antiterrorism task forces were set up throughout the United States. Before long large numbers of suspected terrorists had been detained for questioning. It was soon evident that bin Laden's plan had extended to U.S. targets abroad. Plots against European targets were revealed as well. There were arrests in England, Belgium, France, Spain, the Netherlands, Germany, and Canada.

Some of the names and faces were new, but the tactics were strikingly similar to those used in bin Laden's previous exploits. The suspected ringleader of the September 11 attack was a man named Mohamed Atta. Atta, a member of the Egyptian Islamic Jihad, was just one of at least nineteen people involved in the terrorist mission. A number of these individuals had remained inconspicuously in the United States for some time. Several had learned to fly at American flight schools. To deflect suspicion from themselves, they deliberately behaved in ways an Islamic fundamentalist would not. These men were clean-shaven, had gym memberships, and wore cologne. They even bought cigarettes and went to strip clubs.

On an international level, President Bush made his demands crystal clear. Bush insisted that the Taliban turn over bin Laden and those members of al Qaeda residing in Afghanistan. "Make no mistake," the U.S. president promised, "the United States will hunt down and punish those responsible for these cowardly acts."[2] True to his word, Bush had already taken steps to build a strong international coalition to stop bin Laden and his followers. The alliance would be crucial militarily. It would also choke even more tightly bin Laden's international cash flow.

The Bush administration was keenly aware of just how hard eliminating bin Laden might be. During Bill Clinton's presidency there had been a number of unsuccessful secret agreements with other nations to put an end to bin Laden. It was also later publicly revealed that for the past three years small bands of U.S Special Forces had been scouring Afghanistan in search of bin Laden. In addition, the U.S. had been secretly sending teams of American officers to Afghanistan to confer with Ahmed Shah Massoud. Maasoud was the head of the Northern Alliance, an Afghanistan resistance group, which had been actively fighting the Taliban. The United States wanted Massoud's forces to try to either capture or kill bin Laden.

However, all such attempts failed, and two days before the September 11, 2001, attack, bin Laden had Massoud assassinated. He sent two suicide bombers posing as television journalists to do it. Bin Laden knew that the United States would be more likely to openly embrace the resistance fighters after September 11, and he wanted to render the group leaderless.

Despite enormous pressure, the Taliban continued to protect bin Laden. The regime was willing to go to war to do so. The Taliban was actually safeguarding a legend as well as a man. Bin Laden had long been of value to their cause both as an inspiration and as a leader. Many in the Taliban idolized him. On October 7, 2001, the United States began bombing raids on

Taliban military targets, making it highly unlikely that either the Taliban or Osama bin Laden would last indefinitely.

Nevertheless, there are those who say that Osama bin Laden will admirably serve the Islamic fundamentalist revolution dead or alive. Sudan's Islamic religious leader Hassan al-Turabi, who remained a close friend of Osama bin Laden, described the phenomenon this way: "They [U.S. leaders] have developed Osama bin Laden as a champion, as a symbol of Islam for all young people in the Muslim world. Even if they reach him and kill him, they will generate thousands of bin Ladens, thousands of them."[3]

If this is true, the United States may face a still greater challenge in the future. Dispelling the myth is likely to be even more difficult than toppling the man. Although the United States and its allies have pledged to root out bin Laden's international terrorist following, that may prove to be a herculean task. It is true that heroes often become even more popular in death. So in one way or another, Osama bin Laden may be with us for some time to come.

# Source Notes

CHAPTER 1
1. N.R. Kleinfield, "A Creeping Horror," *The New York Times*, September 12, 2001.
2. Juan O. Tamayo, "U.S. Suspects Mideast Group Planning Attacks in America," *The Miami Herald*, February 10, 1999.
3. Michael Daly, "Bin Laden has Cheated Bomb Attacks for Years," Knight-Ridder/Tribune News Service, August 22, 1998.

CHAPTER 2
1. Yosef Bodansky, *Bin Laden: The Man Who Declared War on America* (Rocklin, CA: Prima Publishing, 1999), XIV.
2. Ibid., p. XV.
3. Ibid., p. XIII.
4. Radical Islamic Fundamentalist Update: A Newsletter Reporting and Analyzing Current Events and Developments, vol. V., no. 3, May 1999.
5. ABC News, "Crime and Justice—Target America: The Terrorist War," January 14, 1999 (transcript).
6. Edward Girardet, "A Brush with bin Laden on the Jihad Front Line," August 31, 1998 www.csmonitor.com/durable/1998/08/3/[/19sl.htm
7. Jan Goodwin, "Buried Alive: Afghan Women Under the Taliban," OTI (On the Issues), Summer 1998, vol. 7, no. 3, Web page, July 2, 1998.
8. Ibid.
9. Ibid.

CHAPTER 3

1. Simon Reeve, *The New Jackals: Ramzi Yousef, Osama bin Laden and the Future of Terrorism* (Boston: Northeastern University Press, 1999), p. 159.
2. Ibid.
3. Ibid.
4. Ibid., p. 160.
5. Yosef Bodansky, *Bin Laden: The Man Who Declared War on America* (Rocklin, CA: Prima Publishing, 1999), p. 10.

CHAPTER 4

1. Simon Reeve, *The New Jackals: Ramzi Yousef, Osama bin Laden and the Future of Terrorism* (Boston: Northeastern University Press, 1999), p. 161.
2. Ibid.
3. Yosef Bodansky, *Bin Laden: The Man Who Declared War on America*, (Rocklin, CA: Prima Publishing, 1999), p. 14.
4. Ibid., p. 17.
5. Reeve, p. 168.
6. Scott Macleod, "The Paladin of Jihad," *Time*, May 6, 1996, p. 51.
7. Bodansky, p. 10.
8. Reeve, p. 166.
9. Ibid.
10. Ibid.
11. Ibid.

CHAPTER 5

1. Simon Reeve, *The New Jackals: Ramzi Yousef, Osama bin Laden and the Future of Terrorism* (Boston: Northeastern University Press, 1999), p. 170.
2. Ibid.
3. Ibid., p. 171.
4. Ibid., p. 172.
5. Yosef Bodansky, *Bin Laden: The Man Who Declared War on America* (Rocklin, CA: Prima Publishing, 1999), p. 36.
6. Ibid., p. 44.
7. Reeve, p. 174.

CHAPTER 6
1. Yosef Bodansky, *Bin Laden: The Man Who Declared War on America* (Rocklin, CA: Prima Publishing, 1999), p. 36.
2. Ibid.
3. Simon Reeve, *The New Jackals: Ramzi Yousef, Osama bin Laden and the Future of Terrorism* (Boston: Northeastern University Press, 1999), p. 174.
4. Bodansky, p. 62.
5. Ibid.
6. Ibid., p. 65.
7. Ibid., p. 68.
8. Ibid., p. 70.
9. Ibid., p. 72.
10. Ibid., p. 76.
11. Ibid.
12. Ibid., p. 77.
13. Ibid., p. 80.
14. Scott Macleod, "The Paladin of Jihad," *Time*, May 6, 1996, p. 51.
15. Reeve, p. 182.
16. Ibid.
17. Bodansky, p. 89.

CHAPTER 7
1. Yosef Bodansky, *Bin Laden: The Man Who Declared War on America* (Rocklin, CA: Prima Publishing, 1999), p. 102.
2. ABC News, "Talking With Terror's Banker: An Exclusive Interview with Osama bin Laden," (John Miller, correspondent) May 28, 1998 (transcript).
3. CRS Report for Congress, "Terrorism: Middle Eastern Groups and State Sponsored," Updated August 9, 1999.
4. Bodansky, p. 110.
5. Ibid.

CHAPTER 8
1. Yosef Bodansky, *Bin Laden: The Man Who Declared War on America* (Rocklin, CA: Prima Publishing, 1999), p. 137.
2. Ibid.

3. Scott Macleod, "The Paladin of Jihad," *Time*, May 6, 1996, p. 51.
4. Simon Reeve, *The New Jackals: Ramzi Yousef, Osama bin Laden and the Future of Terrorism* (Boston: Northeastern University Press, 1999), p. 184.
5. Ibid.
6. Ibid.
7. Ibid., p. 185.
8. Ibid., p. 186.
9. Ibid.
10. Ibid., p. 187.
11. Bodansky, p. 181.
12. Reeve, p. 193.
13. Bodansky, p. 190.
14. Ibid.
15. Ibid.
16. Reeve, p. 194.
17. Ibid., p. 195.

CHAPTER 9
1. ABC News, "Crime and Justice—Target America: The Terrorist War," January 14, 1999 (transcript).
2. Simon Reeve, *The New Jackals: Ramzi Yousef, Osama bin Laden and the Future of Terrorism* (Boston: Northeastern University Press, 1999), p. 200.
3. Ibid.
4. ABC News.
5. Christopher Dickey, Gregory L. Vistica, and Russell Watson, "Saddam & Bin Laden?" *Newsweek*, January 11, 1999, p. 36.
6. Ibid.
7. Stephen J. Hedges and Lisa Anderson, "Grand Jury Charges bin Laden, Associates in Embassy Bombings," Knight-Ridder/Tribune News Service, November 5, 1998.
8. Fact Sheet: Steps Taken to Serve Justice in the Bombing of U.S. Embassies in Kenya and Tanzania, Released by the Office of the Spokesperson, U.S. Department of State, August 1999.
9. Steve Thomma and Richard Parker, "Clinton Bans U.S. Transactions With bin Laden," Knight-Ridder/Tribune News Service, August 22, 1998.

10. Ibid.
11. Ibid.
12. Tim Weiner, "U.S. Says Afghans and Bomb Suspect Have Fallen Out," *The New York Times*, March 4, 1999.
13. Dickey, Vistica, and Watson, p. 36.
14. Fact Sheet: U.S. Conterterrorism Effects Since the 1998 U.S. Embassy Bombings in Africa, Released by the U.S. Department of State, August 7, 2000.
15. Jack Kelley, "Afghanistan Refuses to Turn In bin Laden," *USA Today*, November 12, 1999.
16. Ibid.
17. Ibid.
18. Jeffrey Goldberg, "Inside Jihad U.," *The New York Times Magazine*, June 25, 2000, p. 36.
19. Ibid.

CHAPTER 10
1. Rahimullah Yusufzia, "Wrath of God (Osama bin Laden)," *Time International*, November 11, 1999, p. 16.
2. Elisabeth Bumiller with David E. Sanger, "In Speech, Bush Says Terrorism Cannot Prevail," *The New York Times*, September 12, 2001, p. A1.
3. Simon Reeve, *The New Jackals: Ramzi Yousef, Osama bin Laden and the Future of Terrorism* (Boston: Northeastern University Press, 1999), p. 202.

# Glossary

**Allah**  Muslim word for God

**al-Qaeda**  terrorist organization Osama bin Laden helped to develop

***Al Quds al-Arabi***  Islamic fundamentalist newspaper

**famine**  severe, widespread food shortage

***fatwa***  decree from an Islamic leader or Islamic court that carries the weight of law

**FBI (Federal Bureau of Investigation)**  branch of the U.S. Department of Justice, which investigates all violations of federal law

**financier**  person skilled in or involved with financial affairs

**Horn of Africa**  area on the eastern tip of Africa that is vital to international shipping

**house of al-Saud**  Saudi Arabia's ruling family

**International Islamic Front for Jihad Against Jews and Crusaders**  broad, anti-Western terrorist coalition

**jihad**  holy war

**kingpin**  person of pivotal importance

**Koran**  the Muslim holy book

**mosque**  Muslim temple of worship

**mujahideen**  holy soldiers or fighters

**mullah**  Islamic religious leader

**Operation Restore Hope**  U.S./UN humanitarian aid mission to bring food and medical supplies to Somalia

**propaganda** any widespread effort to promote an idea, opinion, or course of action

**protégé** person aided in his or her career by an older or more experienced person

**Shiite** branch of Islam

**Stinger** powerful, heat-seeking ground-to-air missile

**Taliban** extremist Islamic regime

# Further Reading

Ferber, Elizabeth. *Yasir Arafat: A Life of War and Peace.*
Brookfield, CT: Millbrook Press, 1995.

Foster, Leila Merrell. *Afghanistan.* Danbury, CT: Children's Press, 1996.

Gaines, Ann. *Terrorism.* Philadelphia, PA: Chelsea House, 1999.

Gruber, Ruth. *Exodus 1947: The Ship that Launched a Nation.*
New York: Times Books, 1999.

Herda, D. J. *The Afghan Rebels: The War in Afghanistan.*
Danbury, CT: Franklin Watts, 1990.

Jamieson, Alison. *Terrorism.* New York: Thomson Learning, 1995.

Landau, Elaine. *Land Mines: 100 Million Hidden Killers.* Berkeley
Heights, NJ: Enslow Publishers, 2000.

Nardo, Don. *The Persian Gulf War.* San Diego, CA: Lucent
Books, 1991.

Ramsay, Hank, and Elsa Marston. *Women in the Middle East.*
Danbury, CT: Franklin Watts, 1996.

Rodenbeck, Max. *Cairo: The City Victorious.* New York: Knopf,
1999.

Schroeter, Daniel J. *Israel: An Illustrated History.* New York:
Oxford University Press, 1998.

Spencer, William. *The United States and Iran.* Brookfield, CT:
Twenty-First Century Books, 2000.

Stefoff, Rebecca. *Saddam Hussein: Absolute Ruler of Iraq.*
Brookfield, CT: The Millbrook Press, 1995.

Swisher, Clarice. *The Spread of Islam.* San Diego, CA:
Greenhaven Press, 1998.

Williams, Mary E. *The Middle East.* San Diego, CA: Greenhaven
Press, 1999.

# Index